STUMBLING INTO
GRACE

"Writing with a wisdom and compassion informed by her own vulnerabilities, Mary Pezzulo helps us to recognize need when we see it, and then shows us how to apply the Christian Works of Mercy, one circumstance at a time. In a world that seems filled with new normals, strange challenges, and more people than ever carrying the heavy weights of illness, poverty, loneliness, displacement, and disillusionment, we may all find ourselves stumbling into grace and feeling ill-equipped as we do. This book is the helpful guide we need to stay focused on Christ, live, and serve within a world that is very different from the one most of us were born into."

Elizabeth Scalia
Editor-at-large
Word on Fire Catholic Ministries
Author of *Strange Gods*

"In *Stumbling into Grace*, Mary Pezzulo invites you into a robust spiritual and theological initiation into each corporal and spiritual work of mercy. Pezzulo's gift as a writer is to educate through bold narrative, and after reading this book you'll never think about giving a drink to the thirsty or instructing the ignorant in quite the same ways. This is an excellent resource for both committed and searching Catholics who want to live out their faith through the incarnate mercy of Jesus Christ. Pezzulo is a provocative and trustworthy guide for just such an adventure."

Timothy P. O'Malley
Director of McGrath Theology Online
McGrath Institute for Church Life
University of Notre Dame

"So many books on spirituality seem written from a distance, usually from on high, or from the vantage point of suffering endured but comfortably now in the past. Mary Pezzulo's writing is, blessedly, nothing like that; it sings with the immediacy of what Johannes Metz called the 'painful experiment of living.' We need more work like hers, rooted not just in the ideals of our faith tradition but in the lived experience of Catholic women, to accompany us on the spiritual adventure of being human. This book itself is a work of mercy."

Jessica Mesman
Associate editor of *The Christian Century*
Author of *Love and Salt*

"A deeply personal, raw encounter with the Works of Mercy. Mary Pezzulo's insights are not only emotionally moving and inspirational, they are also intricately relatable and practical for most everyone's everyday life."

Fr. Casey Cole, O.F.M.
Author of *Called: What Happens after Saying Yes to God*

STUMBLING INTO
GRACE

HOW WE
MEET GOD IN
TINY WORKS
OF MERCY

MARY PEZZULO

Ave Maria Press AVE Notre Dame, Indiana

Founded in 1865, Ave Maria Press is a ministry of the United States Province of Holy Cross.

www.avemariapress.com

Paperback: ISBN-13 978-1-64680-063-6

E-book: ISBN-13 978-1-64680-064-3

Cover image © peeterv / iStock / Getty Images Plus.

Cover and text design by Samantha Watson.

Printed and bound in the United States of America.

Library of Congress Cataloging-in-Publication Data
Names: Pezzulo, Mary, author.
Title: Stumbling into grace : how we meet God in tiny works of mercy / Mary Pezzulo.
Description: Notre Dame, Indiana : Ave Maria Press, [2021] | Summary: "In this book, the author instructs readers on living the works of mercy while describing their redeeming power during tumultuous periods of her own life"-- Provided by publisher.
Identifiers: LCCN 2020055001 (print) | LCCN 2020055002 (ebook) | ISBN 9781646800636 (paperback) | ISBN 9781646800643 (ebook)
Subjects: LCSH: Corporal works of mercy. | Spiritual works of mercy. | Christian life--Catholic authors.
Classification: LCC BV4647.M4 P49 2021 (print) | LCC BV4647.M4 (ebook) | DDC 248.4/82--dc23
LC record available at https://lccn.loc.gov/2020055001
LC ebook record available at https://lccn.loc.gov/2020055002

This book is lovingly dedicated to the volunteers at the Friendship Room in Steubenville, Ohio, and to everyone else who has helped me find Christ when I was in darkness.

CONTENTS

INTRODUCTION

Listening to the gospel reading at Mass one day, I realized I hadn't failed after all. I'd felt like a failure for a long, long time. I thought I had failed at everything I set out to do.

I had come to Steubenville, Ohio, to study for a master's degree in philosophy at Franciscan University. My undergraduate degree—from a secular college in the town where I grew up—was in English with a concentration in writing, but I felt I didn't have anything to write about. I wanted to learn something worth writing on. Franciscan University had such a strong reputation for holiness and orthodoxy in the circles where I dwelled at the time, so I was sure I could learn all there was to know there. With this master's degree I'd be a professor and a bioethicist and write all kinds of compelling things to bring the enemies of the Church to their knees. I was full of fire, passion, and naiveté; I was going to learn all there was to learn to teach people, save lives, and win souls for Christ. All I had to do was stay the course and study hard, and God would show me the way.

Of course, I couldn't stay the course. And there I was fourteen years later, still in Steubenville. The gospel reading at Mass that day was from Matthew 11. Jesus asks the crowd about his cousin John, "What did you go out to the desert to see? A reed swayed by the wind?" (v. 7).

Steubenville had been nothing but desert for me—a dry and barren wilderness. First, I had a series of medical emergencies and surgeries, combined with some nastiness that ended with me cutting ties with most of the community in which I grew up. Then I met Michael, and we fell in love. We married in the big baroque Catholic church downtown. My health got worse and worse until I was finally diagnosed with fibromyalgia, a chronic neurological illness causing nerve pain, fatigue, anxiety, and digestive issues. I couldn't finish school no matter how hard I tried because of the extreme fatigue caused by my illness. Michael had to drop out of school to take care of me.

I had some embarrassing and even traumatic experiences with a priest and some students at Franciscan University, which made it feel awkward even to be on campus. Then I got pregnant unexpectedly, and our daughter was born. We found ourselves unemployed, living in a slum apartment on a very bad street in a bad part of town, with no job prospects, no friends, and no hope. We were trapped.

In the gospel, Jesus kept up his questioning: "Then what did you go out to see? Someone dressed in fine clothing? Those who wear fine clothing are in royal palaces" (Mt 11:8).

I was wearing fine clothing, by my standards, just then. I had sent away for a gently used "new" outfit and a brand-new scarf to wear to church. Nice clothing was a pleasant change in our lives, as for years we'd had nothing nice to wear. I felt that I had seen nothing nice at all. The city of Steubenville is a grim, cruel, lonely place in so many ways. I felt that I'd seen no beauty for more than a decade. And yet I had. I had seen glimpses of the most glorious beauty—the kind of beauty you don't see clearly unless you've been trapped in ugliness for a long, long time.

I had seen beauty that time somebody helped us. The time I got a chance to help somebody, and for a change I'd taken it, instead of missing the opportunity as I usually do. I'd seen beauty in the friends I'd met downtown at a little hospitality house called the Friendship Room, where the poor are welcomed, and in the way those people welcomed me.

Again Jesus asked, "Then why did you go out? To see a prophet? Yes, I tell you, and more than a prophet. This is the one about whom it is written: 'Behold, I am sending my messenger ahead of you; he will prepare your way before you'" (Mt 11:9–10).

A prophet is a mouthpiece. A prophet is someone who tells you what God has to say, who shows you the things that God wants you to see.

What have I seen since I've been here? I've been through some cruel things that would make you feel as though the love of God wasn't real at all. But I've also received mercy through the hands of other people, and that mercy showed me that the love of God is real. I've seen so many places that lacked love—places where God was shut out in favor of selfishness, including in my own heart. I've seen so many terrible injustices I hadn't known existed before.

I have also seen people who, in the face of cruel injustice, tried hard to help others. I've seen how one little spark of kindness can dispel a whole world of darkness. And I've wanted, more than anything, to be a part of that light. I have learned so much about darkness and how light can push it back. I have so many ideas about how to help people and how to make a difference now that I've seen what needs there really are. I didn't have any idea before.

When I started my blog at Patheos, I didn't expect to speak about poverty and abuse so often, but now that's what I'm known for. And I have so many stories about how people have fought back to help the poor and the abused, the people our social structures, systems, and networks tend not to see or, worse, deem worthless.

I realized that day as I listened to the gospel that I have discovered the mercy of God in the very way he meant it to be discovered—through the mercy of people. I've found God again and again in my own life when I've been helped and when I've been able to help other people.

After Mass, I went outside into the hazy late evening, which had already grown dark. The mist was rising off of the noxious, polluted Ohio River, and the near-perpetual December rain was falling. The whole world was wet, gloomy, and cold, but I felt warm.

I had come out to this wilderness to learn about God so that I could teach others. I tried to learn about God from textbooks and teachers. I dropped out of school due to sickness and was in darkness for a long, long time. But along the way, I learned about God. I learned about God in the Works of Mercy. I discovered what I should have known all along—that God comes to us through others when they care for us, and that we bring God to others when we care for them. I stumbled into the grace of understanding that of all the ways God can choose to come to us in the pain and suffering of our day-to-day lives, he loves most of all to come to us through people.

I found the thing I came out to see after all. I wanted to see the living God, and I found God living in us, with us. Emmanuel, God with us, is here in the dark, ugly mist and the cruelty of Steubenville, Ohio. He is here in the people who need our help: "For I was hungry and you gave me food, I was thirsty and you gave me drink, a stranger and you welcomed me, naked and you clothed me, ill and you cared for me, in prison and you visited me" (Mt 25:35–36). And God is here for us in the love of other people—even in this world so terribly dark and so often seemingly empty of love. I have something to say about

God after all. God is present in the Works of Mercy, and I can
show you how.

1.

FEED THE HUNGRY

For a time, we were very, very poor. I thought that time would never end. It had started soon after Rosie was born; I was sick, and Michael could not find work anywhere. It's a unique hell being almost done with a master's degree and then not being able to go back to school because your wife is so sick. The cheap jobs don't want to hire you for fear you'll leave for something for which you're better qualified, but the good jobs don't want to hire you because you're not qualified yet.

As for me, my health was fair one day and terrible the next. I had developed fibromyalgia, perhaps due to a series of emergency surgeries I'd had. First my appendix ruptured, then a few months later I suffered a bowel obstruction, and then my gall bladder needed to be taken out the following year. I'm told people often develop fibromyalgia after a series of physical traumas to the body like that. Fibromyalgia has been recognized as a chronic medical condition for only a relatively short time, and we're still not sure exactly how it happens or how to fix it. When I was first diagnosed, many doctors still thought that it wasn't real, it was all in my head, and I was crazy. I almost believed them.

When I got pregnant unexpectedly, I went into remission for a time. I'm told that it's also common for some chronic illnesses to disappear under the influence of pregnancy hormones. Then Rosie was born via traumatic caesarean section after a horrific twenty-seven-hour labor with a con artist posing as a midwife. As he was cutting me open, the doctor laughed at me for trusting the locally known swindler. Post-traumatic depression settled in not long after our daughter's birth. When the pregnancy hormones began to wear off, the fibromyalgia came back.

We had no money, no job prospects, no hope. We were living in a dilapidated apartment building on a dreary street in a bad neighborhood, separated from friends and most of both of our families. We paid the rent with a small check my grandmother sent monthly as a gift. We lived off food stamps and very little else.

There was not enough to eat. Every month I tried to carefully plan meals in advance, but I was never quite prudent enough. We bought sacks of brown rice, canned beans, whole bony chickens, and the most boring frozen vegetables. We would eat the chicken for two or three meals and then boil the bare bones for an insipid, fat-free stock we used for cooking the rice to give it a little more nutrition. I dreamed about having choices again, of the luxury of fast food or even a sit-down restaurant.

Once, in a month when we were especially poor, a neighbor gave us a box of food. We had done her a favor once upon a time, returning her phone when we found it on the ground where it fell out of her purse, so she returned the favor by helping us out when she got a job. She was working at a thrift store that didn't have a license to sell food, so when someone mistakenly donated a big box of food, she passed it along to us. It was mostly canned vegetables, which we went through quickly, but there were also three sacks of ripe potatoes. I didn't even know potatoes could get ripe. I thought they just slowly inflated with water and carbohydrates under the ground and then stayed dry and rocklike until you cooked them. But potatoes do ripen and then they rot, and rotten potatoes stink. These potatoes were close to rotting.

We worked at those potatoes. We ate them baked and boiled and scalloped. I spent some of our monthly government benefits on butter and sour cream to make the most of them. But there were only three of us, and we could not eat three sacks of potatoes faster than potatoes could age in our humid kitchen.

We found ourselves with something that we hadn't had in a long time: more food than we could eat before it spoiled. Meanwhile, downtown, my friend Molly found herself with the opposite problem: a big crowd of people to feed and nothing to give them to eat.

There was going to be a polar vortex. Most of the time, in winter, it's miserable outdoors in Steubenville at night, but the temperatures stay in the twenties or thirties. You could survive living outside if you slept during the day and stayed moving all night. It would be painful but not deadly. And there is a homeless shelter to sleep in, though it's a dangerous place, and showing up early enough to get a bed is tricky if you work, as most homeless people do in Steubenville and everywhere else. But the polar vortex was predicted to bring the temperature down to far below zero, even during the day. Frostbite, they said, would start within ten minutes. Death would come soon after that for anyone unfortunate enough to be outside.

Molly and her husband, Bill, made arrangements with the owner of an after-school program for teenagers downtown. Since schools were going to be closed during the polar vortex, he wouldn't need his building for the after-school get-togethers, so he handed the keys to Molly and Bill for them to use it as a temporary warming center to help the homeless survive.

Molly and Bill had even less of an idea about what they were getting into than I did when I first came to Steubenville to study philosophy. From the moment they opened their temporary shelter, Molly and Bill had far more guests than they'd expected. Many of them were homeless, but not all. It turns out that there were a lot of people living in Steubenville who had housing, technically speaking, but were vulnerable to the cold anyway. There were people who had a house or apartment but the furnace was broken and the landlord couldn't be bothered to have it fixed. There were people who had a working furnace but couldn't afford to pay an old utility bill and the gas was shut off. There were also people whose houses depended on an oil furnace but they'd run out of fuel oil for the winter and couldn't afford more. All these people had been nailing blankets over the windows, sleeping in their coats, and hoping for the best. When they found out there was a warming center in town, they flocked there for shelter and stayed all night.

In addition to people with no housing and no working furnace, Molly and Bill's one-night makeshift warming center was also visited by Steubenville's prostitutes. These women were used to being outside on the street all day. They had never before had a place downtown where they were welcome to duck inside, enjoy a cup of coffee, and get warm for free. They even had friendly hosts to talk with.

None of these people brought their own lunch, of course. So Molly got on Facebook and asked friends to bring her a coffee maker, a teapot, a hot plate, and something for everyone to eat. And that was how it all began.

The polar vortex came and went. Michael, Rosie, and I hunkered down in our apartment, and Molly and Bill passed out hot drinks and bowls of soup and tried to keep order at the crowded warming center. When it was over, they realized they just couldn't leave all these people in so much suffering after befriending them for a weekend. So they decided to open the warming center nightly, after the children from the after-school program had gone home, just until spring came.

Molly got on Facebook every few days that winter, asking for warm food to share with her unexpected party. She started setting her posts to public without even thinking about it. Before long, total strangers were showing up at the warming center: strangers who brought her paper plates and bowls; bags of salad; fruit; and slow cookers of soup, stew, and chili. And I wanted to help so badly.

One of the most painful parts of being poor is feeling that you don't have a purpose. Everyone wants to feel helpful, but poor people don't have a lot of material goods to contribute, and it can make a person feel like a burden instead of a member of a community. I would have loved to be one of the helpful neighbors bringing food and dishes to the warming center. But I didn't have any paper plates and bowls, or any money to buy them. I didn't have any soup, stew, or chili. And I didn't have the means to make them. But I had potatoes.

I knew I couldn't just bring the warming center raw potatoes. Molly didn't have an oven in the building. But I didn't have a whole lot of ingredients to bake a casserole or make a stew. At the beginning of the month I'd have had canned milk, onions, and stock to make a potato casserole of some sort, but at this time of the month I only had beans, rice, those potatoes, and one package of sour cream I hadn't gotten to.

The potatoes were going to be ruined if I waited more than a few days to do something with them. Then I thought about how comforting it can be to open up a nice baked potato on a cold day, and that was my inspiration. I threw the potatoes in the oven and baked them; then I stuffed them in an insulated bag, packed a separate bag with the tub of sour cream, and took the potatoes downtown on the bus. Thankfully the bus wasn't very crowded—a hot sack of potatoes needs its own seat and I couldn't have afforded the fare—and the driver let the potatoes ride for free.

When I got to the warming center, I opened the bag, and there was that rush of warm air I'd imagined sharing with cold, hungry people. I set ten warm baked potatoes on the counter. They were all eaten within minutes.

I felt happy the rest of the day—as if I really belonged somewhere. I'd really been able to contribute to other people's comfort and happiness. And at the same time, I felt guilty for being so happy. The potatoes hadn't been purchased by me, after all. They were a gift in the first place. I just exposed them to heat.

But then it occurred to me: potatoes are always a gift. There's never been a potato that wasn't a gift. To some people, God gives land and the means to grow potatoes. To some, he gives money and access to stores or restaurants. To others, he sends a sack of potatoes through a friend. But food is always a gift from God. The rest of us just help pass it around.

This is the state we live in as human beings. We live in a world full of resources, full of good things to eat. Plants and animals that can be made into food are all around us, and all of them are gifts from God. But these gifts are not distributed evenly. That's the part of the job God left for us. And there are multiple different ways we have to do this. We certainly ought to participate in politics and do our best to make a world where few go hungry in the first place. But the poor are always going to be with us. We're always going to end up with people in our community who just need someone to bring them something to eat. And that's good. That's a mercy that God has given to us.

Think about all the ways that food factors into our lives—not just as nourishment for our bodies but for the cultural, psychological, and spiritual realms of human life as well. Imagine how cranky you get when you're hungry, and how good it is for your mental health to indulge in a treat during a stressful time. Think about the joy associated with a turkey at Thanksgiving and a lamb or a ham with boiled eggs on Easter Sunday. Think of the fasts and abstinence we observe at different times in the Church to remind us of the necessity of repentance. Imagine the myriad foods associated with Christmas and how the feast looks different in all the diverse cultures where Christ is worshipped: special breads and cookies, a feast with seven kinds of fish and myriad pastas, turkey and plum pudding, tamales, fried chicken.

Remember how privileged we are to have the Holy Eucharist. God could have shared his own being with us any way he wished, but he chose this one: a sacred ritual starting with bread and wine, two foods nearly every culture has in some form. He nourishes our whole being in the most intimate, scandalously loving way—through a meal.

Food is not only a physical necessity. It nourishes our whole being—mind, soul, and body. We live in a world full of food, but that food is not evenly distributed. That's our job. Giving food to hungry people is a sacred privilege, because when we give others food, we get to help God complete creation. We get to take the gifts he created to sustain us, his children, and give them to the people he meant to sustain. We feed their whole beings, not just their stomachs. It's a simple and primal way to make another person feel part of a community, to feel welcome and cared for. And it's so often a joyful thing for the giver as well.

How to Feed the Hungry

- Feeding the hungry doesn't have to be an expensive or lengthy activity, but it should be a thoughtful one. Even if you're only making a quick meal for a family member, you shouldn't do it on autopilot, because what you're doing is sacred. When you feed someone, you're fulfilling your vocation as a human being and a Christian, just as a priest fulfills part of his vocation when he celebrates Mass.

- In general, the needier the person you're feeding, the more care you should take. If you're throwing a dinner party for well-to-do friends, they can always get another meal on the way home if they don't like what you served, but poorer friends might not have that luxury. If you're packing a lunch for your spouse to take to work and they don't like it, and if they have the money, they might just buy another lunch. But if you pack a lunch for a homeless person, it might be the only thing they get to eat all day, whether they like it or not. So be extra careful. Every time you feed someone, you perform a Work of Mercy. But feeding the neediest people should be done with the most care.

- If you would like to perform this Work of Mercy by giving to a soup kitchen or food pantry, the most useful donation is usually cash. That way those who manage the place can shop for what they need. If you'd like to donate food, their most needed items are usually shelf-stable proteins such as beans, canned fish, and shelf-stable milk. They also can usually use wholesome snacks such as granola bars, produce such as cans of low-sodium vegetables, and shelf-stable juice with no corn syrup. If you don't know what they need at a given time, you can usually call and ask. Donate brands you'd eat yourself; don't be cheap just because people are desperate.

- If you would like to give something to a beggar you meet, some people don't like to give cash. If you are one of them, you could keep a few gift cards to local grocery stores, gas stations, or fast-food restaurants in your wallet to give away. If you see the same person asking for help often, you might offer to take them to lunch or grocery shopping. Or you could bring them a lunch. If you give them food, make sure it's nourishing and appealing, something you'd like to find in a packed lunch yourself. Bear in mind that they might not have a place to keep food refrigerated. Also remember that a lot of very poor and homeless people have bad teeth, so soft fruit such as peaches or bananas might be more welcome than apples. Snacks with lots of sharp bits such as nuts and sunflower seeds are harder to eat than crackers and peanut butter.
- Please don't ever give away expired or recalled food. A food pantry can't give that away and the soup kitchen can't cook it, so you've just made more work for them. And if they don't catch it and accidentally give it to someone, you may have made someone sick. Remember, the Gospel of Matthew tells us that the people we feed are Christ in disguise. Give him your best food—food you wouldn't be ashamed to serve to a dear friend.

Food is a sacred gift that nourishes us in every aspect of our being: body, mind, and soul. It's a pleasure that is intimately wound up in our cultural experience. There is food everywhere, but for many people it's not readily available. It's our job, as the hands and feet of Christ, to change that. To feed the hungry is to take part in God's work of creation. It's a simple act, a joyful one, and it binds us in a powerful way to our community. That is a gift we should all be grateful to accept.

Lord Jesus,
You are the bread of life and the source of all
    sustenance.
Please help me to serve you in my neighbors
    who are hungry.
Help me remember that in doing so, I am only
    a servant
joyfully arranging a banquet you have already
    prepared.
In your most holy name I pray.
Amen.

2.
INSTRUCT
THE IGNORANT

I learned about the beauty of the Sacrament of Penance when I was sitting in the ugliest confessional in the ugliest Catholic church I'd ever seen.

Franciscan University's Christ the King Chapel is an architectural nightmare, if you ask me. It's set up in a series of concentric squashed ovals, like the layers of a deformed onion. The outermost layer has a good number of windows to let in the light, and it's where the eucharistic chapel, a foyer, and the offices are. The second layer is just a skinny hallway with two rows of metal coat hooks lining its walls. This is where people stand for Mass if they're late and the seats are all taken up; it means that latecomers spend the entire Mass in a torture chamber where they can't lean on the walls for fear of being impaled. The center is the actual chapel. It's a dark place with only one window of tacky stained glass. The walls are drab, itchy stucco. The benches are black, arranged in two-thirds of a circle facing a dank sanctuary and altar. The lighting is yellow and dim; it makes the priest's vestments look dirty no matter the liturgical season.

Against the back wall of Christ the King Chapel, in that dark middle layer, is a door to what looks like a broom closet but is actually a confessional. Most of the confessions at Franciscan University are whispered face to face in the black pews, but this confessional has a free-standing screen in it, with a chair for the priest on one side and a chair for the penitent on the other. It also has a third chair, inches from the priest's eyebrows, if you change your mind at the last minute and want to go face to face. Other than that, it's just a drab, musty, itchy-walled room with a triangular floor and a nauseating pink fluorescent light. Aesthetically speaking, it would make a better interrogation room than a confessional. It seems designed to make penitents nervous.

I didn't want to be in that confessional for any longer than I could help it. I didn't want to go to Christ the King Chapel at all. I had many bad memories of crying in that place after I'd first come to Steubenville. The living situation I'd gotten away from in my hometown wasn't a good one. I came from a community I loved but that taught a lot of superstition and cruelty along with their catechism, and I wasn't on speaking terms with many of my relatives for that reason as well as other things. When I found myself poor, chronically ill, and without relatives to go home to, I expected I could turn to the Catholic community at Franciscan University. But I quickly found that people who had been my friends blamed me for being sick: *You must be doing something wrong or you'd have gotten better by now. You're a burden. You're faking it for attention.* And besides, I'd had a horrible experience with one of the priests there—one I'll write about in a future chapter.

But it was Sunday, and we didn't have a car or a friend to give us a ride, and I was the closest to healthy I'd been in weeks.

I had had a miserable time sick at home, unable to go out; the flare-up had just subsided that weekend. I walked to Mass with Michael, pushing Rosie in the stroller. I got to sing hymns and listen to the readings and receive Holy Communion for the first time in a long while.

I was glad to see that the priest saying Mass was not the bully I'd encountered previously but a kindly older priest. It was Michael who suggested that we wait awhile after Mass was over and talk to him when he came out of the sacristy. And we did.

Michael explained to the priest that I was chronically ill and we didn't have a car, so I'd been trapped at home. I hadn't been to Confession or received the Anointing of the Sick for an embarrassingly long time. We didn't have a priest friend we could ask, or anyone to bring us to campus during scheduled Confession times. Could he help?

The priest ran to the office to get oil, and then he came back and welcomed me into the ugly confessional. "You've already received Communion. Now, I'll hear your confession and then we'll let Michael in to pray with us while I anoint you. Then you'll have all three!"

I usually go to Confession behind the screen, but I didn't see the point when I'd already been talking to the priest face to face. I sat across from him in the ugly room and recited the list of my transgressions of the past few months. And there was something else that was gnawing at my peace of mind.

When I meet a priest for Confession, I'm not the kind of person who randomly volunteers information unrelated to my sins. Some people seem to like to talk to the priest about whatever's on their mind. I rattle off a list of all my sins as best I can and get out of there quickly. But that day, I kept feeling as though I should mention to the priest something that wasn't a sin. I knew that this priest was a theology professor who was said to know his field very well. I knew he'd be able to give me a straight answer if I confessed to something that wasn't exactly a sin but was a worrying preoccupation of mine.

"I want to offer my suffering to Jesus," I said. "It gives me a lot of peace to do that. But I'm also afraid. Because when I was growing up . . . well, they taught me that if you volunteer to offer your sufferings to Jesus, he sends you more suffering and makes things as bad as they can, so you can offer it up. He makes you his victim soul and tortures you to trade your suffering for other souls. And that makes me afraid to offer it up."

The priest smiled gently. "Nope," he said, with absolute certainty. "That's definitely not how it works."

At one level I'd already known that. A God who was Love couldn't possibly be a sadist tormenting random chronically ill people in order to satisfy his anger with somebody else. That would make him a cosmic abusive boyfriend rather than pure Love. The eccentricities I'd been raised with were somebody's pet superstitions and not Catholicism. Michael and I had talked about this dozens of times. But still, the fear remained. I never felt safe saying any kind of prayer that united my suffering to Christ's, even though I obediently recited prayers to that effect all the time. But when that priest said "Nope," a weight fell off of my shoulders. I felt calm and protected. It seemed as though, somehow, everything was going to be all right.

It wasn't just that the priest was a knowledgeable man who had studied theology. It was also that he was absolutely confident and perfectly gentle when he said it. His confidence was contagious, and his gentleness was soothing. I felt able to accept what he said because of the way that he said it.

The priest gave me absolution and opened the door for Michael. Michael sat in the extra chair as the priest gave me the Anointing of the Sick. I know that great graces were conferred in both of those sacraments, but I'd felt the healing happen when the priest said "Nope. It definitely doesn't work like that." Just at that moment, the ugly confessional in the ugliest church in town seemed like the most beautiful place in the world.

It seems to me that it's a little more delicate to talk about the spiritual Works of Mercy than the corporal ones, because there's a different kind of trouble a person can get into when they try to perform the spiritual works. If you give food to the hungry and drink to the thirsty badly, at worst you leave a person still hungry or thirsty or sick from your terrible cooking. You shouldn't do that. But if you are careless or don't know what you're doing when you attempt a spiritual Work of Mercy, you might end up hurting someone in a deeper way.

The soul is the deepest, closest, most intimate part of a person. The soul is the enclosed garden where Christ always dwells within a human being, whether they can feel him there or not. In the most real way, nobody can hurt another person's soul; only you can hurt your own soul by deliberately committing a sin. But in another very real way, a person can feel their soul to be hurt and can find that relationship with Christ damaged at the level of their personal experience. That person can *feel* too ashamed of themselves to be comfortable speaking to God; they can *feel* that God must not love them and that they are unworthy. They can conclude that God must not be real at all, because he has been represented to them in a foolish or abusive way that doesn't match with their experience of anything good or loving.

A person can become traumatized by their religious experience when people they ought to have been able to rely on for friendship, counsel, and spiritual advice were cruel to them instead of being good and loving. This cruelty runs the gamut from unkind words and bad advice to gossip that ruins somebody's reputation to shunning and even to physical or sexual abuse presented to the victim as having something to do with religious practice. Think of a child badly beaten by an abusive parent who thought they were "training them up in the fear of the Lord." Think of all the horrible cases we've learned about in recent years where a priest abused somebody sexually and claimed it was God's will or the victim's sin that made it happen.

Spiritual abuse is the term for abuse of any kind that damages a person's experienced relationship with God. It's a particularly toxic and traumatic type of abuse because it meddles with a person's experience of the deepest part of their own self. And especially in this era in our Church, with so much terrible abuse committed by our shepherds coming to light, we have to be absolutely clear and honest about the prevalence of spiritual abuse and how damaging it really is. Spiritual abuse can be committed by anybody in a community of believers. It's painful, damaging, and traumatic to be a victim of spiritual abuse. Although the victim feels and might be told that they are shameful and dirty for having suffered, it's never the victim's fault.

One of the common ways I've found in which a person can commit spiritual abuse, without even knowing they're doing so, is by attempting to perform a spiritual Work of Mercy but getting it terribly wrong. Fortunately for us, a spiritual Work of Mercy that's performed correctly is one of the ways in which God heals the effects of spiritual abuse—not all at once, not without the more specialized help of a counselor or a psychiatrist, but as part of a victim's journey of healing. And so every time I talk about a spiritual Work of Mercy in this book, I am going to mention some ways in which a person might be abusing somebody by performing something that looks like a Work of Mercy but isn't. And I'm going to try to show how the Work of Mercy performed in the right way can be healing.

The people who catechized me—and the people who taught them the faith—abused me when they taught me that Jesus was abusive. They didn't mean to do that. They were teaching me what they thought was Catholic teaching, but it wasn't. It's true that in the Catholic faith we believe that our suffering is redeemed through Christ. Christ comes to suffer with everyone who suffers, uniting them to his own Passion on Calvary so our suffering becomes an intercession on behalf of all and for each person without our even having to consciously intend it at every moment. In doing so, Christ turns a bad thing that he doesn't intend—suffering—into a source of great grace.

Saints who suffered especially badly found immense grace in that suffering and thanked the Lord for it. But their words are often misused by unscrupulous teachers who tell people that God *wants* us to suffer and that suffering itself, rather than the redemption of suffering, is a gift from God.

I was traumatized and more than a little scared of Jesus when I was told the untruth about him—that he would make me his victim soul and torture me to trade my suffering for other souls. But I was healed when I was told the real truth—"Nope. That's definitely not how it works."—by a good and compassionate priest in an ugly confessional.

This is one example of how performing the Work of Mercy to instruct the ignorant in the wrong way is abusive, but done in the right way, it's beautifully healing.

Notice how the priest who reassured me was in the middle of doing everything else he could to be helpful—he wasn't just setting out to find an ignorant person to lecture. He was gentle, which was why I had the courage to ask him in the first place. He was well informed and confident, two reasons why I trusted his answer. And he was glad to tell me the truth, and that gladness was contagious. Helpfulness, gentleness, being informed, speaking with confidence, and joy in telling the Good News are all necessary for performing this Work of Mercy.

How to Instruct the Ignorant

- No one expects you to go stand on a box and shout the Gospel at strangers or walk door to door and try to get someone to talk to you. Some people seem to think that's what "instruct the ignorant" means, so I have to get that out of the way first. Shouting at strangers about Jesus or knocking on their door uninvited is an off-putting and scary way to teach others, and being scary doesn't work. There are much better ways to teach.

- Be sure you're being as loving and helpful as you know how to be to your neighbor in the first place. No living human you'll meet is just a disembodied soul; they're a whole person with a mind, a soul, and a body, and all of these are loved by God and important. Besides the fact that it's not charitable, it's disingenuous and off-putting to preach at someone with whom you have no relationship at all. Be active in helping people. Form good relationships just because people are worth knowing. This will cultivate relationships in which questions of faith might come up naturally. And then when they do come up, you can be a trustworthy person to help them understand the faith. That's usually the best way to go about it. Never pretend to be somebody's friend just for the purpose of preaching at them, because that's not honest or respectful of them. It's also an impractical way to teach the Gospel. Love people because they're worth it, and conversations about what you believe will come up in time.

- Your church probably has a catechetical program for children or an RCIA program for adults to teach them about our faith. This is a big undertaking and they could surely use extra help. See if you can help out as a volunteer teacher if that's your gift or an assistant who makes sure that the classrooms are organized and welcoming and can help to keep order with children. If you don't feel that you could help as a teacher or an assistant, you might be able to help by providing drinks or snacks for the meetings, by watching the teacher's children, or by offering some other help to free them to focus more on teaching. Everyone who helps to teach or hand on our faith in any capacity is performing this Work of Mercy, even if they're not the ones doing the teaching.

- When you teach, remember to be gentle! Nobody likes to be treated harshly, and harshness doesn't help a person learn. Harshness hurts people, which is bad in itself, and it makes people less likely to listen to you. Always approach a teaching moment in the gentlest, most compassionate way you can. This way you teach not only with words.

- Don't patronize. Nobody is ever completely ignorant, and nobody on this earth knows everything. Assume that the person you're talking with is a real human being with a whole lifetime of experience to share. Engage them in mutual respect.

- Be informed. Our faith is an enormous, challenging thing to learn. In one way, it's all so beautifully simple; but in another, there are so many different teachings that it can seem overwhelmingly complicated. No one knows it all, not even the best-trained theologians. Read the Bible and the *Catechism of the Catholic Church*, and read them prayerfully, asking the Holy Ghost for wisdom instead of just reading them through like a textbook. Take advantage of any Bible studies or adult education courses your parish might offer, but remember to do your own research. Nobody knows it all, and often teachers bring their own experience and prejudices to the lessons.

- Have confidence and be joyful when you tell the Gospel. Remember: *Gospel* means "Good News." Sharing our faith isn't a morose, scary thing. We're not running around yelling at people that they're going to hell. We're telling them something wonderful that should be a relief to know: Jesus is here to heal us and set us free. If you don't feel confident or joyful about the faith, that doesn't mean you're a bad Catholic. Everybody goes through periods of doubt and difficulty in their spiritual journey; the greatest saints did and so will you from time to time. Just take some more time to study and pray about your difficulties, and perhaps consult with a trusted spiritual director about them. Keep praying and informing yourself so that you can inform others.
- If you're a victim of spiritual abuse, you may find the thought of sharing and teaching the faith daunting. That's normal and not your fault. Don't be afraid to focus on your own healing, if that's what you need in this season of your life. No one can do everything.

We need to teach the truth joyfully and not manipulatively, in a way that respects and loves the whole person. We need to make sure that we ourselves are informed of the truth and that our relationship with God is on strong footing as we approach this spiritual Work of Mercy.

O Jesus,
teacher and healer of my soul,
Thank you for the beauty of the faith!
Please help me to learn the truths you have
revealed,

so that I may be your instrument by instructing
and healing my neighbors, ever sharing with
    them your love.
I ask this in your holy name.
Amen.

3.
GIVE DRINK TO
THE THIRSTY

It was a hot, humid, sunny afternoon in late May and our apartment was about to get its water shut off. I'm told that Steubenville has some of the most expensive tap water in the country, despite the fact that it rains all the time. This is because of pollution. Steubenville is an old steel mill town on the Ohio River, the most polluted river in the United States. The air around here used to be so polluted that it turned the winter snow black, and all that soot and steel dust went right into the soil and the water table.

When I first moved here and lived in a dormitory, the water coming out of the tap smelled like rubber and gave us dry skin after showers. Most of the students bought cases of spring water at the grocery store every week rather than drink the tap water, because it gave us stomachaches when we did. When I moved into my first apartment, I soon gave up trying to get the tub and toilet to look clean; the water itself left rusty streaks on the porcelain. But shortly after I married Michael, Steubenville's utility department put in an expensive filtration system. Suddenly the water tasted good and left my stomach feeling fine. But the price nearly doubled.

Everyone in town was stuck with an astronomical monthly water bill, and the city started sending shutoff threats every single month to those who were behind, even if we were just a week late. We had just gotten our monthly three-figure bill and shutoff notice, and we didn't have a cent to pay it.

Different municipalities have different rules. As far as Steubenville is concerned, there were programs to give poor people a reduced rate on their heating and electric bills. We were on both of those programs, paying only ten dollars per month for each. But there was no such program for water. The water bill had to be paid to the city utility department in full by the beginning of the next week, including the late fees, or we would be shut off. If we were shut off, the landlord would evict us. We would be homeless with a toddler who might get taken away by Child Protective Services until we could find another place to live. This is something that happens when you're poor.

Every state works a little differently, but at the time, Ohio had a special rule to help stop a utility shutoff if there were children in the home. The Department of Job and Family Services could pay off all or most of a water bill in shutoff as long as you only applied once per year and jumped through a number of bureaucratic hoops. One of those hoops was having in hand three rejection letters from three different agencies, stating that we'd asked them for help and been turned down.

This program and its rules were well known all over town. You just had to walk into an agency and say "I need a rejection letter," and a receptionist would grab a pre-printed one off of a stack, write your name on it, sign it, and give it to you without question. The only inconvenient thing, besides the agony of waiting at Job and Family Services to see if you'd successfully applied, was that these agencies were spread all over downtown.

We didn't have a car. We had to take the bus downtown and then walk.

Michael and I had both noticed that when he went downtown to ask for help, the employees at the agencies treated him suspiciously, as if everything was his fault. But when I went downtown, they treated me like a helpless woman who'd had some bad luck, and they were more eager to help. I was having a pretty good fibromyalgia day, so we agreed that I would go downtown by myself and he would watch the baby.

I started at one end of Fourth Street and walked all the way down to the other, more than a mile, so I could hit three agencies before showing up at the Department of Job and Family Services. The day kept getting hotter and more humid, and I was not dressed for hot weather. I'd worn the most respectable outfit I could put together out of my thrift-store clothes, so I'd look grateful, humble, and clean-cut for the various agencies.

I'd forgotten to pack a bottle of water to drink while I walked. And I didn't have any money to buy a drink. Eventually I needed to sit down, but there were no benches to sit on in that part of downtown. Benches encourage vagrants, after all, and the businesses didn't want any of those. So I ended up sitting on the pavement in the shade of a brick building behind a Chinese restaurant, and then I was too dizzy from the heat and the thirst to get up again.

I gazed at the traffic zipping back and forth down Washington Street, fantasizing about drinks. I could almost taste a clean glass of ice water; I could hear the crisp noise of opening a can of orange soda. I would have given anything for a bottle of that odd blue sports drink that's supposed to taste like raspberry but actually just tastes like sugar and dye. I wanted all of these drinks, and I could have none of them.

I was visible to the drivers buzzing past, physically speaking. I was a solid object in their line of sight. I could see them, and they could see me. But I wasn't visible in another way. I was a poorly dressed person sitting on the pavement, looking listless. That meant that respectable people in cars were trying not to look at me, without thinking that that's what they were doing. That's what we're all brought up to do when we see a poor person sitting where they shouldn't be sitting—we ignore them and mind our own business. We do it without even thinking about it. Poor people sitting on the side of the road are invisible because of a culture that tells us we're not supposed to look. But the Gospel demands that we stop that. We have to look. We have to be attentive to the plight of our neighbors and make them our business again.

I fantasized about the cars stopping, just as I'd fantasized about drinks. I imagined somebody pulling over, opening their car door and helping me up, then helping me into the cool of an air-conditioned vehicle. I imagined them asking how I was, and my telling them my trouble. I fantasized that they would help me complete my errands by car and then take me through a drive-through for a nice cup of soda or ice water. But, of course, they didn't.

Thankfully I was rescued. Molly and Bill and several other volunteer friends of theirs had closed up the temporary warming center now that it wasn't cold anymore. The owner of the after-school program needed the building during the day, after school let out. A building where teenagers go to stay out of trouble after school isn't an ideal location for prostitutes and people struggling with addictions to show up asking for help. But the volunteers couldn't just abandon all the homeless and near-homeless people they'd befriended during the winter. The poor face great challenges when the weather is warm as well.

In summer in urban areas where there aren't a lot of trees and greenery to break up the pavement, heat pockets form. It can be much hotter in a block of cheap apartments surrounded by blacktop than it is in a manicured neighborhood with grass and shade trees. And poor people might not be able to pay their utility bills in the best of times, even with programs to reduce the rates, so using electric fans and air conditioners might be completely out of the question—even if they could buy fans and air conditioner units in the first place. With the high price of water, these people weren't going to indulge in a nice long cold shower or fill a wading pool either. Some couldn't even afford the bus fare and entry price to use the municipal pool in another part of town.

And those were the poor people who had houses or apartments. Homeless people suffered much more. And people who struggle with addictions often have trouble balancing their electrolytes just from the drugs they take. Now, sweating outside all day, they were in even more danger of a medical emergency.

Someone donated an old building to the volunteers to use as a cooling center, but they found the building was in unsafe condition, and they couldn't afford to do the repairs that would bring it up to code. So they put up a tent in the building's parking lot. They plugged in a refrigerator to the outdoor outlet. They set up tables, chairs, and a jury-rigged outdoor air conditioner made from fans and blocks of ice. And they served the poor outside, passing out ice pops, drinks, and fruit salad and inviting them to sit in the tent.

That tent was close to where I'd collapsed. And the volunteers who worked there were doing the opposite of what the drivers on Washington Street were doing. They weren't ignoring poor people who looked like they were in trouble. They were actively looking out for us.

A volunteer approached me respectfully. "Ma'am? Would you like a drink?" He helped me up. He brought me to the table beside the big fan. He gave me not only a drink but also a bowl of salad and a hot dog. I opened the cold, sweating bottle of water and took several big gulps. Imagine how good that tasted. Imagine how that mercy felt.

It's hard to overstate how important water is to human beings—not only physically but emotionally and spiritually as well. Try to imagine all of the things you use water for. Think of drinking, cooking, doing dishes and laundry, and flushing the toilet. Think about cleaning your house. Think of the comfort of a nice hot bath, a dip in the pool, or a nice cold shower. Remember how wonderful it is to go on vacation and swim in or boat on the ocean, a river, or a lake. Maybe you love fishing or scuba diving and are thankful for the bounty of creatures who live in water. Think about your flower or vegetable garden and what happens to the garden when there's a drought. Now think about all the food you buy at the store and how the farmers who grow it depend on water.

Think about the priest washing his hands at Mass, the life-giving waters of Baptism, the sprinkling at the asperges. Water is as important to our sacramental life as bread and wine. We can't live without water physically, and the new life of our soul begins with a prayer and water.

Imagine what it would be like if you didn't have access to clean, safe water. More people suffer that way than you think—including right in your own community. Christ suffered thirst with us in his agony on the Cross. One of his seven last words to us was "I thirst." That message of his is rightly often interpreted to have a spiritual meaning—Christ's thirst for souls. And it does mean that. But Jesus was also referring to the physical agony of thirst after bleeding and suffering in the heat for so long without a drink. Christ suffers with everyone who is thirsty. Every time we help someone have access to the clean water they need, we are comforting Christ.

How to Give Drink to the Thirsty

- Don't neglect the opportunity to offer drinks to people who drop by for a visit. This is a simple way to honor and love them. Have water or lemonade in the fridge for company, and keep coffee or tea on hand on cold days.
- Does your community have a program available to help poor people pay their water bills and avoid shutoff? If so, be sure to support it when you can. If not, this might be a good thing to arrange with your city council or state legislators, or it might be a charity you can found, if you have the time and resources. Doing so would be a huge help to many people.
- Remember that every time you give somebody a drink, you are comforting Christ. This is true even if it's a simple chore such as pouring glasses of milk for your family's dinner or bringing juice boxes to a Little League game. Be grateful for these opportunities and do the chores as joyfully as you can.
- Whenever you can, donate to organizations such as Paper for Water that provide clean water and plumbing to poor people. This can be a great charity to support with a parish, school, or youth group fundraiser.
- Having access to clean water depends on having a clean environment in your own community and all over the world. Practicing good stewardship of the environment is another way in which we safeguard. Many communities already have groups of concerned citizens working to improve the local watershed—that is, the land around a body of water, the places the rainwater drains out of into rivers and streams. Get involved with one and see how you can help. Maybe your friends, parish, or youth group can organize a day picking up litter on a local beach, or donate

to a charity that protects the wetlands and marshes that keep our water supply cleaner. There are a lot of issues to consider when you vote, shop, and dispose of your garbage, but don't neglect considering the environment as well. Caring for the environment is one way we care for human beings.

- In summertime, keep a small cooler with chilled bottled water in your car to hand out to anyone you meet who is asking for help.
- Be sure to check on your poor, disabled, and elderly neighbors and friends. Make sure they're not having trouble paying the water bill every month. If you can help financially, you should. But at least be there to offer a ride, moral support, or bus fare if they need to trek downtown and try to beg agencies for help.

Water is not just a physical need. Clean, beautiful water is also necessary for mental and spiritual well-being. It's something that sustains and heals all of us. Human life depends on having access to water. We can help our neighbor have access to this beautiful grace when we practice the Work of Mercy of giving drink to the thirsty.

Heavenly Father,
Your Son suffered terrible thirst in his agony
    on the Cross.
Help us to comfort our neighbors who also
    thirst
for clean water, for safe homes, for fair
    treatment.

Thank you for the gift of water and the
     opportunity
to help safeguard all the natural resources you
     have given us.
I ask this in your most holy name.
Amen!

4.
COUNSEL
THE DOUBTFUL

I spend an embarrassing amount of time on social media. This is how I got to be a blogger in the first place. I am sick at home for so long so often that the only friends I talk to regularly are online. I meet with my friends online for role-playing games in private groups. I chatter about my day with people on Facebook. I belong to forums and groups on this or that topic, including some for people who have been spiritually abused. In 2016, Sam Rocha, the editor of Patheos Catholic, noticed that I wrote carefully thought-out treatises in replies on Facebook and asked if I'd like to have a blog, and I've been blogging ever since.

I know a lot of lapsed Catholics. We belong to a lot of the same forums and groups. I think I may have more lapsed Catholic friends online than practicing Catholics. This doesn't surprise me at all, because I am friends with so many people who have been abused. When you've been abused in the name of our faith, it's very hard to see any of the good in it. Our faith is not a book of rules and regulations. It's meant to be spread through mercy and love, from person to person. Put abuse into the equation and the Good News of the Gospel starts to look like a lie. In that particular context, it is a lie. A person who abuses others while pretending to practice Christianity professes to be acting in the name of Christ while doing what the devil would do. They're living a lie. Christ isn't a lie, but that person's Christianity is.

I don't know if, in writing this, I come off as a very faithful person or not. But I can't even tell you how many times I've had a bad day or a particularly difficult argument with a fellow Catholic, said "I give up," and felt like our faith was nothing but a manipulative fantasy. Once, I had such a hard time that I actually said, "I can't call myself Catholic anymore," and I didn't receive Communion for several weeks. I kept going to Mass, though. It didn't feel right to stay home on a Sunday when I wasn't sick. Every time the priest held up the host I'd say, "If you are God, I love you." And I admitted to friends I was talking to on social media that I actually did believe and profess what the Church taught. It was only that I was so horrified by the way people had treated me at Franciscan University and back in my hometown that I didn't believe God could come through the hands of such people.

Just a short time after that admission, I found myself in a Confession line. I confessed everything and stayed for daily Mass and received Communion, and then there I was, a practicing Catholic again, almost without knowing how I'd gotten there.

That was the worst struggle I've had with the faith. There have been others. When the horrific Pennsylvania grand jury report was released in 2018, I was so disgusted that I went through a time when Catholicism seemed like a lie. I wandered into Mass and said my daily prayers more like a person reciting lines than a believer.

There are days where I have terrible darkness and doubt and don't feel Jesus could be a real person. If he were a real person, would he have left me here for so long and let things get so difficult? And so much worse for so many other people? But I keep coming back to the faith, and I think that that is the Holy Ghost working in me. It's *someone* I'm being drawn up into rather than *something* I consciously hold on to.

I was raised to believe a person was supposed to take a hard line on doubt. You weren't supposed to allow yourself to dwell on what you didn't know and on what didn't seem true. You were supposed to force yourself to believe by sheer willpower. And you were never, ever to ask impertinent questions.

I had a brother who was a lot smarter than I was. He was full of questions. He was always interrupting evening prayers and catechism lessons to ask, to insist, to express doubt, and to say when things didn't make sense. This horrified people. They said he had a "rebellious spirit." A person who was charged with teaching us, a woman I'll call Hannah, spiritually abused my brother by treating him like a reprobate and a lost cause, all because he wouldn't let her get away with reciting the catechism at him unchallenged. He wanted answers, logical answers, and that offended her. She spiritually abused me by acting as if my beloved brother was going to hell for doubting and questioning. She actually told me, "If your brother goes to hell, remember that you'll still be perfectly happy in heaven." And she said that in front of my brother. I prayed fervently to save my brother. I used to stay up late at night panicking, afraid that God would really throw an inquisitive little boy I loved deeply into a lake of fire to punish him. That woman traumatized both of us.

I think I act in reaction to what was done to me and my brother every time I'm in an internet forum talking with someone who used to practice Catholicism and doesn't now. I don't think of the beauty of our faith first of all. Rather, I feel what it's like to be a terrified child, begging a God who doesn't seem loving not to throw a little boy into hell.

I have come to see our faith differently. The Catholic faith is not something you have to force yourself to believe without question or you'll go to hell. The faith is a person who dwells within us, even when we can't feel his presence, and that person is Christ.

Christ is someone who loves us, sometimes through other people, sometimes in spite of them—indeed, sometimes even when they are acting in ways that makes him look like a monster. Christ was also abused by members of his own faith, after all. He was abused by both spiritual and civil authorities. Christ is someone who suffers with us, saying *"Eloi, Eloi, lama sabachthani?"* (My God, my God, why have you forsaken me?) on that terrible Cross when we can't manage to believe just now because it's so dark.

We worship a God who also had a crisis of faith in a way. In one sense, he was omniscient and already knew everything at every time while he was with us on Earth as a man. But in another, he allowed himself to feel all of our helplessness and blindness in his Passion. That was just as real. All of human doubt is folded into that *"Eloi, Eloi, lama sabachthani."* Christ wasn't just saying "Why have you abandoned me?" for his own self. Christ was also suffering my frustration and saying, "Why have you abandoned Mary?" and my husband's frustration, saying, "Why have you abandoned Michael?" and my daughter's, saying, "Why have you abandoned Rose?" and my brother's, saying, "Why have you abandoned him?" That is my experience of Catholicism. That's what I try to bring with me whenever I'm talking to somebody about the faith.

I still feel that I'm portraying myself as way too pious. I'm no saint. When I'm bantering with my friends on social media, I'm often irreverent and silly. I swear too much. I'm not careful

to control my temper and sometimes I lash out at people. Sometimes, in secret groups, I vent in a very mean, salty way about
my frustration. I express my doubt and other people express
their doubt to me.

Some of my friends are atheists who don't practice any faith
at all anymore. However, they are very good, loving, and ethi-
cal people, so sometimes I tell them I don't think they're really
atheists. We both believe in and work for love, kindness, justice,
and mercy. I believe that those are attributes of God, and they
believe differently about them, but we both know they're real
and bigger than we are, and we work to serve them. That doesn't
sound to me like not believing in a deity. I also have friends
who call themselves "hopeful agnostics." They are cynical about
any organized religion because they've seen how abusive the
members of organized religion can be. But they believe there
must be a force ordering all of this somehow, and they live lives
honoring whatever or whoever that is. I respect and love those
friends very much.

I often meet people who don't know what to believe, and we
find ourselves in a very sacred, delicate place, a kind of limbo
where people are free to admit that they just don't know. That
place is called "doubt." And doubt is scary.

Once, I don't remember how long ago, maybe even before
I was on Facebook, somebody in an internet forum mentioned
being estranged from an abusive family and feeling very alone.
They wanted to pray but weren't sure how when they didn't even
know if there was anyone listening back for them.

I had a hundred memorized catechism answers for just such
an occasion. I had scripted arguments I'd learned in apologetics
lessons on the tip of my tongue. But those all felt so disingenuous and cold. Here was a suffering person, not a character in
a script. I wanted to be gentle. I wanted to say something that

would respect their spiritual journey, comfort them, and give life.

I didn't even know if it would hurt that person to say "Jesus" or "Christ" to them. I ended up saying, "I'm so sorry that happened to you. I've been abused too, and I am estranged from most of my family. I think that a good thing about the Divine is that the Divine is so big that they can go on being real even if we can't believe right now."

And that seemed to help. I was very glad I helped that person and so glad that I'd said that. Because before I'd said it, I didn't even realize it was true. The good thing about God is that God is so big that he can go on being real even if I feel like I can't believe in him right now. Even if no one believes, God is still real. When I doubt, the life of God is still in me.

Doubt means wondering if something you're supposed to believe might not be true. We doubt all the time. It's how we think critically, take risks, make choices, and learn. Sometimes we doubt certain things we've been told to believe, question them, find that they were false, and stop believing them. The general rule of thumb is to not plant any seeds until after Mother's Day so that they aren't killed by frost. However, I doubted that there would be another killing frost one spring because the weather had been so mild—or at least, if there was one, it wouldn't kill the seeds I put in the ground, only the seedlings. I turned out to be right. Seedlings put in the ground before Mother's Day would be too early and get nipped by the frost, but seeds take a couple of days to germinate and could be planted early. My doubt led me to learn something different from what I'd been taught.

Sometimes, however, we're told something and we doubt and question it, only to find out that it is true and our doubt wasn't telling us the truth. I had been told that I could learn to drive with proper lessons, but I doubted it. I didn't feel it was possible. I'm in my thirties. Every time I got behind the wheel I would panic. I felt helpless and too stupid to learn. However, when Rose's godparents paid for my lessons with a good instructor, I started to learn. I got used to it. Now I know how. My doubt was unfounded. I can learn to drive.

Doubt also happens with spiritual things. We experience doubt, and sometimes we decide that that means the things we were taught are false. But we also experience doubt, and we still have faith during and on the other side of it. Doubt itself isn't losing faith. It's part of the journey of faith. When we doubt, we can ask questions and figure out what we really believe.

Doubt is a thing that happens to every human. Even Jesus on Calvary felt as though God had abandoned him, and Jesus was omniscient. He knew very well that there could never be a place where God was not. But he felt doubt that it was true, and he said so. He expressed his doubt, his fear, and his frustration. This means that doubt isn't a sin. It's just something that happens. Often it happens because someone has misrepresented the faith to us through their actions and made it look like a lie. But other times, it just happens for no reason.

When a person doubts their faith, they can become afraid. It's scary to not know what to believe. This can be compounded if the person in doubt is a victim of spiritual abuse. They might have had an image of God represented to them that had nothing to do with a God of love. They might have been told God was strident and wrathful and would toss a little child into hell if the child had questions. They try to believe in such a God because they think they have to force themselves to be confident—and I'm sure the real God, the God of love, is pleased that they're trying to love him even while he's pained that they find him so scary. And now, here they are experiencing doubt, which is normal. This doubt could lead them to reject the false, scary image of God and embrace a God of love. But they don't know that, so they treat the doubt like a fault of theirs. Or perhaps they surrender to the doubt entirely instead of taking it under advisement and discerning what they really believe. They start not believing in God at all.

Our faith teaches us that counseling the doubtful is a Work of Mercy. It's something we're supposed to do to bring the mercy of God to our neighbors. But we have to be very careful not to hurt someone who is in a place of doubt, because doubt is scary. The place of doubt is a place where a person needs to be comforted and gently advised—not bullied—so they can make their own choices.

How to Counsel the Doubtful

- Please be advised that this Work of Mercy isn't called "order the doubtful around" or "make the doubtful feel bad about themselves." It's about counsel, and counsel is gentle and respectful. You wouldn't go to a professional counselor who yelled at you for the hour you paid for. Don't counsel someone by being harsh. Being harsh with someone experiencing doubt is wrong because it's cruel. And it's also just not helpful. The Gospel is the Good News of the love of God. You can't reassure someone of God's love in an unloving way. That's not how the message is spread. Love is spread by love, and gentleness by gentleness.
- People are not objects we can control, nor are we meant to control them. Counsel isn't about forcing someone to listen. It's about respectfully telling them something that might help in their spiritual journey. Before you can counsel the doubtful, you have to accept that what they do with your

advice is up to them, not you. In that place of freedom and peace, you can counsel.

- If you've been spiritually abused, you might have been taught that someone else's salvation is your responsibility. You may feel afraid when someone else expresses doubt—as if God has sent that person into your life as a test, and if you can manipulate them into believing again, you'll pass; but if you can't, then you fail and you'll both go to hell together. God wouldn't do that to you. He gave human beings free will on purpose. Counseling is a Work of Mercy, but you are not going to be punished because of what somebody else does.

- Doubt is not a sin. It's not a sin to have questions, to wonder if something is true, or to look at another faith's spiritual beliefs to see if they're closer to your own. It's not a sin to be at a point in your spiritual journey where you just can't wrap your mind around a certain teaching or see how it could be true. The faith is bigger than any of us. Every one of us will go through patches of our spiritual journey where we wrestle with the truth. The wrestling itself is part of having faith. Doubt is scary and uncomfortable, but it's not evil. It's just something that happens. The first step toward counseling the doubtful is to reassure yourself and be reassuring about this.

- When a person expresses to you that they feel that they're losing their faith, don't jump to correct them or recite the catechism. Just listen carefully. After you've listened, you can ask questions until you're sure you understand what's going on.

- After you've listened and asked questions, it's alright to not have an answer. You can pray for grace and see if you can think of anything that will be helpful. You can recommend a book or a good spiritual director. But it's also okay to say,

"That's hard for me too. I don't have an answer to what you're going through, but I just wanted to tell you that it's normal to feel doubt. God isn't upset that you can't believe right now."

- Another thing you can say is, "Let me get back to you on that." Then you can look the answer up in the *Catechism* or in a good book on apologetics or ask someone you trust, and get back to the doubtful person. Hopefully both of you will learn something. In my experience, it's a lot better to admit you don't know and then go find out than it is to have a memorized script.

- Some apologetics experts seem to think that everybody who doesn't believe in Catholicism is stupid. They'll write a sample conversation you're supposed to memorize and have at the ready, but it's not a conversation with a real person with a journey and a spiritual life. It's a conversation with an idiot who doesn't really exist, for the purpose of making the apologist look smart. I think it's best to stay away from those. Resist the temptation to always have a glib answer on the tip of your tongue. It's better to be honest and empathetic. Christ is love, not a syllogism. Counseling the doubtful is not about making yourself look smart.

Doubt is not a sin, but it is a scary and uncomfortable thing to experience. When we perform the Work of Mercy of counseling the doubtful gently, with understanding and compassion, we can help people through this place to a greater trust and understanding of God. This is a wonderful gift we should all be thankful for. God is bigger than all of us, and we don't have to be afraid of doubt.

Lord Jesus Christ!
Thank you for sharing your doubt with us,
when you felt abandoned on the Cross.
Help me to be a good listener and an honest,
    compassionate counselor
when my neighbors experience doubt.
I ask this in your most Holy Name.
Amen!

5.
CLOTHE THE NAKED

I was at the thrift store again. All my clothes came from the thrift store. We weren't quite destitute at this point, but we were on a very tight budget. This thrift store had a weekly Tuesday special: all adult clothing was twenty-five cents per item, unless otherwise marked. I could afford that.

I looked through racks of gently and less gently used things, all of it perfumed with that odd thrift store antiseptic smell. There were jeans with ragged cuffs, ugly stretch pants with pilling on the insides of the legs, sweatshirts with the names of sports teams I didn't care about. There were sweaters with lumpy embroidery of pumpkins and Christmas stockings. In the middle of the rack, there was a bright red tunic top printed with a colorful design.

Most of my clothes were dowdy and in muted colors. I was conscious that I wasn't very attractive. In fact, I'd been teased for most of my childhood for being unattractive. I'm fat, and my face isn't conventionally pretty. I'd spent most of my teenage years on a diet and trying to find clothing that hid my stomach; the only makeup techniques I knew were about covering blemishes. Most often I felt like I was one gigantic blemish, and

I usually didn't want to be seen. I wore a lot of dark blue and black—when I had a choice.

Lately I hadn't had any choices at all. I bought clothes at the thrift store, clothes other people didn't want. I didn't want them either.

But I liked the colors of that tunic. I liked red. I liked the cut of that tunic. I thought it might cheer me up. I paid a quarter for it, took it home, and put it on. Every time I wore it, people treated me differently. It wasn't that they had been rude to me before—sometimes they were, but not usually. It's just that when I wore the tunic, more people than usual seemed to smile at me or say hello. And the ones who said hello often said, "I like your shirt!" or "You look nice!" as well as just hello.

If you're not often told you look nice, you might not know how odd that feels or how it can make you flush with pride. I was used to being slammed for being ugly if someone commented on my appearance. Suddenly people were telling me I looked nice. I could hardly wrap my mind around that.

I started doing a little research on the internet, "doing my colors" by comparing my skin and hair to models in photographs. I'd always liked colors, but I'd thought of them as things to admire in nature or in paintings. I'd learned some art in college; I'd wanted to be an artist but had been shooed away from studying art as a major because it wasn't practical. My family and the people who taught me the faith were dead set on my being a writer and a teacher. I painted and drew for a hobby. I loved mixing colors of paint or pastel chalk to get a pleasing composition. Sometimes I had even more fun mixing a palette of colored acrylics than painting the actual painting. But I'd never once thought of color as being something that could make me happier with my own body. I'd only thought of hiding my body.

According to the fashion experts, my skin and hair made me a "warm autumn," suited to wearing a warm, rich palette of fall colors rather than blacks or pastels. That was exciting because autumn colors are my favorite. I love gold, aqua, burnt orange, plum, teal, and apple red. Autumn is my favorite season in which to admire nature. I would enjoy wearing warm autumn colors even if they didn't look nice on me.

I started buying clothes in colors that I thought suited me, whenever I could find them at that thrift store on Twenty-Five-Cent Tuesday. I liked the rush of confidence it gave me when people were more respectful and said I looked nice.

I had begun my job blogging for Patheos by then, which meant people were giving me gratuities to live on. In addition, I had a tiny monthly paycheck that was barely more than a hundred dollars. This didn't mean we could support ourselves handsomely or that we didn't still need my grandmother's help, but it did mean that I got a tax refund in late March. When the tax refund came, I badly needed new clothes. Instead of the thrift shop, I went to a local department store and picked out several outfits I could mix and match—all in colors that suited me according to my internet research. I got some lipstick and nail polish that matched the clothes. I also bought a box of dye and dyed my hair a fun shade of auburn. That was a wonderful, healing moment, and it did make my life feel much easier.

I will never forget what it felt like to have nothing nice to wear—or rather, I will never forget what it felt like when I first bought that red tunic top. I hadn't noticed how dreary I'd felt until I saw the difference. I'll never forget what a change it made in my self-esteem to have good clothes.

The word *naked* comes from an Old English word that means "exposed." This was first pointed out to me in a blog post by my friend Mark Shea, another Patheos blogger. But I've also seen other people remark on it several times. The Old

English word is *nacod*. It doesn't just mean "without clothes" but also "exposed" and "vulnerable."

Nakedness can be taken literally in the sense of exposed skin, but providing clothes for a person who is literally naked is not something a lot of us do on a day-to-day basis. If you're the caregiver for a small child or a disabled person, you do. But people often miss that clothing the naked means covering other kinds of exposure and vulnerability as well. Anytime you've felt scrutinized and embarrassed; anytime a physical or other part of you was bare that you felt ought to be covered up, you have been naked.

Think of Christ on Calvary with his clothes ripped off, standing there in front of everyone who mocked him. It wasn't just that he was naked and physically uncomfortable. It was the exposure, shame, and humiliation of nakedness that was traumatic.

People who are very poor are exposed all the time. The worst poverty can't be covered up and hidden. And that lack of a place to hide is shameful, because our culture makes poverty a shameful thing. Not having the means to provide for yourself shouldn't be shameful. It's a fact of life. Everyone starts out helpless when they're born, and we die that way as well. Most people go through at least some of their adult years needing help too, but we're told the lie that that's wrong and that the people who can't hide their need are bad.

Poor people wear that shame in their clothing as well as in their lack of clothing. Think of a homeless person standing outside shivering in inadequate clothes in winter, or forced to wear the same coat all the time because they don't have anywhere to take it off. Think of a person who is overheated and covered in sweat stains in the summer because they don't have appropriately light clothing or enough changes of clothes to get them through to pay day when they can go to the laundromat. Think of someone who can only afford to buy clothes at the thrift store where they might not have plus sizes or tall sizes of clothes or where they might only have sizes that are too big or tall; imagine how awkward that feels, to be constantly adjusting clothing so your stomach or breasts don't spill out. Try to remember what it was like to be a child or teenager who got teased for an outfit at school and then remember that poor children have to wear dowdy thrift store clothes to school every day. Poor people's clothing is the very thing that exposes them to shame—their clothes make them naked.

This is something we can help with when we perform the Work of Mercy of clothing the naked. It's not merely about going out and finding a stark-naked person to cover up. It's about helping people cover what they find shameful and to have a better sense of their own dignity.

Have you ever looked at a picture of Christ being stripped of his garments on Calvary and wished you could do something to help him feel less embarrassed? That's what you do every time you perform the Work of Mercy of clothing the naked.

How to Clothe the Naked

- If you're part of a family that lives together, you probably already perform this Work of Mercy in many ways. If you have a child at home or an elderly or disabled relative that you help to bathe, diaper, and dress, you've done it. Be sure that you help them in ways most respectful of their dignity, since not being totally in charge of such things is embarrassing for children as well as adults. If you're helping a child or mentally disabled adult dress, obviously you can't let them choose every aspect of their wardrobe without limits, but you can try to offer them a few choices you've picked out ahead of time.

- If you're the one whose job it is to do the laundry for your family, you can also do that with an eye to people's dignity. Look at people's clothing as if it were really a part of their sense of dignity, and be conscious and careful about your work. You're preparing clothes for Jesus, after all.

- If you have the opportunity to personally provide some clothes for a poorer friend, it's often much more respectful to take them shopping with you so they can pick out an outfit they like or to give them a gift card to a good clothing store instead of picking out something you hope they like and that you hope fits. Remember, clothing the naked isn't just about putting clothes on people; it's about helping them feel their God-given dignity when circumstances make it hard.

- When you're donating used clothing to the poor, make sure it's clothing of a quality you'd wear yourself. Only give away gently used clothes that you don't want but wouldn't be ashamed to wear if you had to. Don't give away useless, torn, and ugly things that no one would want to wear if they didn't have a choice, unless you're giving to a thrift shop you know has a rag recycling program. Otherwise, just throw away the useless clothing yourself.

- Don't give used clothes that are out of season to a shelter or Catholic Worker house unless they've asked you to do so. Most of the time, those places have limited storage and will end up throwing things out. Give away warm clothes in the winter and cool clothes in the summer.

- If your local Catholic Worker house has a Facebook page, check it often. Sometimes a guest will come in with no shoes or nothing to wear, and they'll post on Facebook asking for someone to drop off some new clothes or shoes of a certain

size. You can bring clothing to them that you know they'll
be able to use right away.

- A lot of homeless people really need socks, and having new
socks can be a good way to help them feel better. If you're
preparing a lunch or a care package for a homeless person,
consider including a new package of comfortable socks.

- Some people have a good habit of packing a gently used
purse with hygiene supplies, gift cards, and snacks to hand
off to a homeless woman if they meet one. This is a great
way to help somebody, but make sure it's a nice-looking
purse that isn't shabby. Also, consider throwing in something
extra, such as good makeup or inexpensive earrings. Being
homeless can feel so undignified, and little things like this
can often help her feel loved.

- Consider having a warm clothing drive at your parish or
with your school or youth group. This can be a great Christmas project or a project for after Christmas in the dead of
winter. But don't collect the cheapest winter hats, gloves,
and coats you can find. Make sure everybody knows to bring
things they would like to wear themselves if they had to be
outside all day.

- Donate money to organizations such as Beauty 2 the Streetz
that help the homeless with hygiene and clothing-related
issues to help them feel dignified and loved. Some of these
organizations have wish lists online where you can buy a gift
for a homeless person and have it shipped to them as well.

- Remember that this Work of Mercy applies to restoring a
sense of dignity in anyone who has been exposed or humiliated. You also practice it every time you stand up for or
befriend someone who has been a victim of gossip, discrim-
ination, and prejudice. Be attentive and don't ever miss an
opportunity to do that.

Nakedness is not just physical; it's any state where a person feels embarrassed or exposed. Clothing the naked means restoring that sense of dignity to every part of a person by providing appropriate, comfortable, and good-looking clothing and by protecting people from gossip and prejudice as well. This is something we can do to honor Christ who was so humiliated on Calvary, and that is a wonderful gift.

Lord Jesus Christ
who suffered shame, humiliation,
and nakedness for our sake,
help me to clothe those who are physically or
     emotionally naked
wherever I find them.
Open my eyes to see ways in which I can build
my neighbor's sense of dignity and help her
     or him
feel respected and worthy of love.
I ask this in your most holy name.
Amen.

6.
ADMONISH
THE SINNER

From the time I was in sixth grade until I moved to Steuben-ville, I was a member of a close-knit community that I loved. It consisted of my biological family and also several other deeply conservative Catholic homeschooling families so dear to me that I thought of them as my aunts, uncles, and cousins rather than just my friends. We didn't live near one another, but we saw one another several times a week. We went to the same church. We pooled our resources for a homeschooling co-op and took care of one another if someone was sick or if a mother was having a new baby. We went on field trips and sometimes even on vacation together. I loved that community. There are so many people in it whom I miss. There are so many things about it that I wish I had now.

But there were also some deeply abusive things about the community. This includes the falsehoods I was taught along with my catechism—I've already mentioned that I thought that God was hurting me on purpose to make me offer my suffering up and that people I loved would go to hell. Another was this:

there was a person in that community in a position of authority over me who was responsible for teaching me, and she had a very nasty, abusive mouth. She liked to nitpick, criticize, and call names. I'm not going to use her real name; it's the same person I referred to earlier as Hannah.

Hannah would make fun of my appearance. She would mock me constantly for being pudgy and then all the other children under her authority thought it was funny and did the same. She sat across from me at the table and mocked every bite of food that went into my mouth and then the other children joined in. Hannah once found out that I'd gained four pounds in a two-week period of high stress when I was supposed to be on a diet, and she announced this fact to the whole group to humiliate me. She teased me for my lack of fashion sense. She had a special disdain for my hair, which she was constantly trying to fix for me. She manipulated me into letting her style it and ended up hacking it to bits and scorching it with bad dyes.

Hannah also made fun of everything I liked, because it bothered her that I was a nerd and not outgoing. She liked to tell everyone in the community that I was selfish, narcissistic, and a "diva." She accused me of attention seeking when the stress from constant taunting made me cry. I suffered from extremely low self-esteem growing up, and I still do, partly due to Hannah's constant taunting. But Hannah used my low self-esteem as more evidence that I was broken, and she made fun of me for that.

Hannah had a particularly cruel habit that a lot of abusive people have: she would occasionally try to manipulate me by accusing me of all kinds of horrible faults, and then she would sulk and not speak to me for a while. This was torture because I couldn't get away from her. I was a child, and she was in charge. I would beg her to forgive me, and she would continue to sulk until I was almost frantic before she magnanimously accepted my apology and acted like a friend for a time.

I couldn't properly protect myself from Hannah's abuse because I was a child and she was an adult, of course. But also because I thought that she was performing a Work of Mercy for me. I thought she was admonishing me for my sins. I assumed that Hannah was a woman of God because she prayed in tongues, led the Rosary, and wrote beautiful things about God to share with others. And I assumed that I wasn't favored by God because I struggled with doubt and because I was constantly being told how inadequate I was. So I thought that Hannah's abuse was necessary to teach me to be good. I thought she was forming my conscience by making me feel so awful. I honestly believed, for a time, that the best way to grow in holiness was to take her abuse and let it shame me.

I make Hannah sound all bad, but she wasn't. She was also a fun person when she wanted to be. Sometimes she was downright affectionate with me, and I loved those times. But she was toxic and cruel as well. She almost killed me. I struggled with wanting to die for a long time because of the abuse.

When I moved to Steubenville and got an apartment of my own, Hannah expected to be allowed to pay regular visits to me along with other people from my community. She also called at random times of the day or night even when I told her not to call me during class.

But the spell was broken. I lived alone now, and I had time to think. I was seeing a therapist for the mysterious depression and self-loathing I didn't realize was caused by my life experiences. I was doing pretty well in school, and I was learning that I was capable of doing things for myself. I began to see that Hannah had hurt me rather than helped me.

I put off talking to Hannah far longer than I should have, but finally I wrote her an email. I told her that the way she verbally abused me was wrong, it had hurt me until I felt like hurting myself, and I wouldn't visit her or let her visit me until she got some kind of help. I could have phrased the email more kindly, but I tried to be reasonable.

Hannah was deeply offended. She immediately pitched one of her sulking fits, but I was adamant. I felt guilty about that, especially when Hannah accused me of being unforgiving. "How many times do I have to say I'm sorry?" she demanded, even though she had never said she was sorry.

Hannah reminded me of everything she'd ever done for me and how selfish I'd been. She threatened to tell the whole community about this; she said that they would think I was crazy and come to Steubenville to "check on me." I was genuinely afraid I'd end up being put in a psychiatric hospital.

I wondered if I might be committing a sin. I wondered if God expected me to quietly take the abuse until it killed me, like some kind of ancient Roman martyr. But I knew I couldn't stand to be abused anymore, so I stood my ground. When the lease was up on my apartment, I moved, and I didn't give Hannah a forwarding address. When Michael and I were married, she wasn't on the invitation list. Hannah and I didn't speak to each other for three years.

Shortly after I announced my pregnancy with Rosie, Hannah emailed me asking to bury the hatchet, and I tried talking with her. She even came to visit the baby three times. I began to think that we'd gotten over our differences and would be good friends. But on the third visit, she got offended with something Michael had said and pitched yet another fit. She accused me of hurting, slandering, and abusing her when I called her out for her abuse years before. She told me all about the trauma I'd caused her by moving without telling her and not inviting her to the wedding. She called me names to humiliate me and bring me to heel, but I stood my ground. I told her I couldn't talk to her about this, and I repeated that it was wrong of her to abuse me and call me names.

That time I didn't back down, and Hannah and I haven't spoken to each other for eight years now. I've felt guilty and ashamed about this many times, but now I know there wasn't anything to be ashamed of in those particular actions. Hannah was sinning against heaven and against me when she ridiculed and emotionally abused me. She sinned by spiritually abusing me when she tried to manipulate me by telling me forgiveness meant I had to let her off the hook, that anything else was me abusing her. I'll get into the problem of forgiveness—what forgiveness is and what it's not—later in this book; for now, I'll just say that she was wrong.

In confronting Hannah over her abuse, I certainly didn't do it perfectly, and I'm not even saying I did it well. But when I stood up for myself, I wasn't abusing Hannah. Rather, I was actually performing a Work of Mercy, the same one I'd thought Hannah was performing for me: I was admonishing the sinner.

Admonishing the sinner is a Work of Mercy. The Church in her wisdom tells us that this is something God wants us to do in order to help our neighbor. However, the Church also tells us not to judge—this command is right there in the Bible. We're also warned against rash judgment and jumping to conclusions. Clearly this is a work that's necessary but extremely delicate to get right.

I'm not saying I got it right in my example of my experiences with Hannah. In fact, I can think of a number of ways I could have been gentler. But I am convinced it was right for me to tell her that what she was doing was a sin—and not just because I was protecting myself from abuse. You should always try to protect yourself from abuse, of course. God doesn't want anybody to be abused. But it also was right because people who are doing something sinful are hurting themselves, and it's a Work of Mercy for us to help them stop if we can.

When we sin, we're not just offending God, as if God is a grumpy schoolteacher with an arbitrary set of rules. Most often we're hurting others in our community, but we're always hurting ourselves. We're doing things that cause injury to the kind of person we are on a spiritual level. Human beings are created in the image and likeness of God who is pure love. When we sin and choose not to love, we are scratching and burning up that likeness, starving parts of our spirits that want to be fed. We mutilate ourselves. It hurts us. We might not feel the pain right now, in our earthly life, when so many spiritual things are hidden. But that spiritual pain is real. God doesn't want us to suffer it.

Our Catholic faith even teaches that there's such a thing as mortal sin: a sin that effectively starts killing the soul until the sinner's soul repents and receives absolution. For a sin to be mortal, it not only has to be grave (a very serious matter) but also fully consented to by a person who really understands one's actions. Any mitigating factors such as mental illness or not understanding one's actions can make a grave sin not a mortal one. In fact, no one can be completely sure that any other person has ever committed a mortal sin. But we can state for fact whether an action is gravely wrong or not.

In Hannah's case, she was doing great spiritual and psychological harm, arguably torturing me to death, and I call that a grave sin. On the other hand, I realize she probably had some serious mental health problems, so I don't know that she was committing a mortal sin.

Sin hurts and kills. If we love our neighbor, we'll find a way, when possible, to warn her to stop hurting and perhaps killing herself. But we have to do this with great love and caution if we're going to be helpful rather than spiritually abusive.

For example, you might spiritually abuse someone if you didn't understand the situation but presumed the worst. Imagine somebody chiding a neighbor for committing fornication when they were actually doing something perfectly innocent. Imagine how humiliated that neighbor would be.

You might spiritually abuse someone if you admonished them in the wrong context or in a way that wasn't prudent or tactful. Imagine confronting a friend about an embarrassing bad habit in front of a group instead of alone.

You also might spiritually abuse someone if you admonished them in a cruel way. I used to pray the Rosary outside abortion clinics. I don't do that anymore because I've found that a crowd outside a clinic does more harm than good to the people walking in. I think a few people are called to be sidewalk counselors, and the rest of us should intercede for them and work to support pregnant women in difficult circumstances in other ways. You're free to think I'm wrong about that. But in any case, while I was praying at the clinic, I witnessed all kinds of terrible attempts at admonishment, and I admit I was guilty of some myself. Some people intervening there didn't seem interested at all in counseling and helping those who felt they had to make such a choice. Rather, they would scream through bullhorns to make those coming to the clinic panic and cry. That's not admonishment. That's spiritual abuse. It's cruel, it never changes minds, and it makes the women they're abusing far less likely to ever want to listen to a Christian again. Don't ever do that.

But if we do have an opportunity to help someone who is hurting him or herself make a better choice, we ought to take it—as long as we can do so gently, respectfully, and in a way that really helps.

In the Gospel, Christ confronts people who are sinning. If the person's sin was public and hurting people, he would even call them out in front of others. But in the case of hurting people who were already outcasts, such as the Samaritan woman at the well, Christ was gentle and spoke to her alone. We have to take his example if we're going to admonish people without abusing them.

How to Admonish the Sinner

- Be absolutely sure of what's going on. Never presume you have information that you don't, and don't ever get carried away by gossip you've heard about somebody else. You could end up spreading gossip and badly hurting somebody if you confront them about a sin they're not even committing. Don't admonish someone if you're not certain of what they're doing.
- Remember, what a person does is ultimately up to them. You can't force virtue. In a circumstance where someone is hurting somebody else, you might be able to deflect the attack by running away, using a self-defense tactic, or calling for help. But barring that, you can't force people to stop sinning. You can tell them what you think and offer to help, and that's all you can do. God gave that person free will, and it would be wrong to take it away from them even if you could. If you're not sure about this point, you may end up abusing someone by trying to manipulate them, even if you have good intentions.
- In the Gospel of Matthew, Jesus says that if your brother sins against you, you should first confront him privately; if that doesn't work, you should go to him in the presence of a witness or two; if that doesn't work, you should go to the leaders of the Church; and if that doesn't work, you may treat him as a Gentile or a tax collector (Mt 18:15–17). That passage has been used in any number of abusive ways. But

it points to the fact that we should always involve the least number of people when admonishing someone, so that we don't run the risk of ruining their reputation.

- Notice that Jesus says to treat people "like a Gentile or a tax collector." But he never says to treat a person like garbage. Jesus invited a tax collector to be his apostle and loved him very much. You can still be friends and be kind to people who don't share your faith. In fact, you should.

- Be willing to help someone if you're pointing out something they need to change. Think of the difference I noticed between the sidewalk counselors who were prepared to help and the people who just wanted to scream through bullhorns. Sometimes people make bad choices because they don't think they have any options, so we can help them by giving them options.

- No one is required to do something impossible. If you're pretty sure that someone is not going to stop sinning because you tell them to, you're not required to keep talking. Don't feel as though you absolutely have to walk up to someone and admonish them if you see them doing something wrong, or that God will be upset with you if you can't dissuade them. Often it's not your place to speak up, and someone closer to that person should handle it. Maybe they already know that what they're doing is against our faith, and you wouldn't do any good by repeating the rule they already know. What you can do is go on being a loving friend setting a good example.

- If a person is being abusive to you and hurting you, you ought to tell them to stop if you have any hope that that will work. And if they won't, you have every right to remove yourself from that situation—even if they've manipulated you into thinking the suffering is God's will. Even if they've told you that doing so will "hurt the community" or that they're only helping you to not sin. I understand that sometimes you're trapped and you can't get away. I was in that situation with Hannah for years, and I know it's an impossible, devastating feeling. If you are trapped in that circumstance, know that I am praying for you to find a way out. When you find it, don't be afraid to get away. It's not your job to fix an abusive person. God doesn't want you to suffer at their hands.

Sin hurts, and left unchecked, it destroys the sinner. It's something that mutilates our souls, and God doesn't want us to suffer that mutilation. That's why he calls us to admonish one another when we can. But we have to do this in a gentle, kind, compassionate way that helps people and gives them options, or we will end up abusing them and making matters much worse. If we can perform the Work of Mercy in charity and gentleness, then we will win over our brothers and sisters in Christ.

Lord Jesus,
who gently revealed yourself to the Samaritan
     woman at the well,
thank you for teaching me so lovingly.
Help me to keep those I know from sinning,
and never let me abuse others
while thinking that I'm practicing
     admonishment.
I ask this in your most holy name.
Amen.

7.
SHELTER
THE HOMELESS

It was winter again, and then it was spring. Molly and the other volunteers from the warming center had finally moved out of their summer tent. Donors had pulled together and gotten them a house: a former duplex with a bright-blue door just across from one of the local Catholic churches. They now had a kitchen for cooking meals and a cheerful dining room for serving. They had a washer and a dryer and a shower for weary people to use. They had a pleasant, shady backyard with a garden, a patio, and a place for children to play safely. They had a living room with bookcases and comfy places to sit.

The volunteers named their house the Friendship Room, and I hope they continue serving the poor in downtown Steubenville until Christ returns. They are open seven days a week giving hospitality to everyone who needs it. In addition to sheltering and feeding people, they host movie nights and card games; they hold an annual Memorial Day picnic, a Thanksgiving dinner, and a Halloween party; they carol together at Christmas. In addition to their main house, which I've visited many times, the

Friendship Room has established two safe houses somewhere in the Steubenville area to shelter abused women and former prostitutes. They strive to be a home for anyone who is without one—a place of welcome and hospitality, a place where people are helped to feel loved, not just provided a roof and four walls.

Instead of Molly just posting to her own Facebook page to notify people about their needs, the Friendship Room got its own Facebook page. They update followers daily on the work they're doing, careful to maintain guests' anonymity unless the guests want to use their own names. This story I'm going to tell you was something I watched unfolding through Facebook.

One of the guests who came frequently to the Friendship Room the first year they were in that new house was an older woman I'll call Ruth. Ruth had a mild intellectual disability. She couldn't keep a job, and she didn't have any close family to take care of her. She would stay with a friend or distant relation until the friend or relation needed the room for somebody else, and then she'd be homeless again until somebody took her in. At the time the Friendship Room first opened, she was staying with a cousin. Ruth used to go to the Friendship Room every day and stay for meals and for company; then she'd go back to her cousin's house to sleep at night.

One day she got kicked out of the room she was staying in, and she went to the Friendship Room for shelter for the afternoon. When she got there, the volunteers realized she was sick. The volunteers at the Friendship Room were used to seeing sick people in the damp late winter and early spring, but this was more than just sniffles. Ruth had a bad flu. They drove her to the hospital where she was admitted immediately, and they stayed with her there for several days. Pretty soon Ruth was on the mend. The hospital was ready to release her to continue healing at home, but she didn't have a home to heal in. Where could she go? Would they really release her right onto the street?

Molly and the volunteers were on the phone all day, talking to social workers and landlords around Steubenville. What Ruth needed was a group home, but there wasn't one available, so the Friendship Room was looking for a small studio apartment where she could sleep at night and take a shower, and then spend the day with them. It wasn't easy, but they didn't give up.

Finally, at the eleventh hour, they were able to find her a tiny studio apartment that would take Section 8 housing assistance vouchers. But they weren't done yet. Molly got on Facebook and asked everyone who was following the Friendship Room online to bring things to help them furnish it. They got a bed and bedding, simple dishes, a bureau, a sofa, a television, and some pictures to hang on the walls, all within that final day. They brought them to the apartment and got it ready.

When Ruth got out of the hospital, the volunteers drove her home—home, to her very own apartment for the first time in her life. She had a roof over her head and a warm place to sleep. She had a legal address that was hers. And she still had the Friendship Room to be her family and look after her during the day.

Ruth burst into tears when she saw the apartment: "I can't believe I have a place where nobody can kick me out!"

Have you ever thought about what a gift it is to have a home? A lot of silly, clichéd things have been said about the difference between a house and a home. But think about that in a new way for a moment. Pretend you've never heard any silly pop songs or ridiculous commercials that play on the difference between those two concepts. Just think about what it is to have a house, and what it is to have a home.

What is a house? A house is four walls for privacy and a roof for shelter. A house is warmth in the winter and cool shade from the summer heat. A house is a place to welcome company for parties and get-togethers. A house is safe storage for all your belongings, so you don't have to constantly carry them with you. A house is an address where people know you can be found. A house also provides you with some means of expressing yourself and showing people who you are, with decorating and gardening. A house is a place to pray, eat, sleep, bathe, and change your clothes, all with the reasonable expectation of safety and privacy while you do.

What if all that was taken away? What if you suddenly found yourself without a house—without warmth, cool shade, privacy, safety, a place to express yourself, or welcome your friends? What if you didn't even have a place to put your belongings, so that you had to push them with you in a shopping cart or carry them in a bag? Have you remembered to be thankful for your house lately?

A home takes things even further. A home is not just a building, though that's part of it. Home provides a sense of stability and belonging. Home is a place where you can expect to stay for a long time, not to be displaced and have to constantly find a different shelter. Home is where you know where everything is, because you put it there—or if you lost something, you can expect that you or a member of your family misplaced it somewhere nearby. Home is where the people welcome and accept you, where you can find community and belonging with a group of other human beings. When you feel at home, you have a sense of stability. You feel safe, understood, and loved. Conversely, when you feel far from home, you feel lost, alienated, afraid, and lonely.

Can you imagine what it's like to have shelter but not a home? Maybe you can stay in one person's house on Monday but you have to find another place to live on Friday. Or maybe you're a refugee who's assigned to a camp for a time and then put on a plane to go live in another country altogether. Perhaps you go to the same homeless shelter every night to sleep, but it's not as though you have the same bed or any sense of stability. Maybe you come into your bedroom in the group home or the foster home to find that whoever's in charge has meddled with your things, but you're not allowed to ask them to stop. Perhaps you live in a house with your family but your family doesn't love you and treats you like a burden.

If you don't have a home, I am sorry. You're not alone. A lot of people suffer in this way, and I pray that you find your home soon.

Christ suffered with the homeless: he himself said, "Foxes have dens and birds of the sky have nests, but the Son of Man has nowhere to rest his head" (Mt 8:20). If you have a home, have you remembered to thank God for that home lately?

Having a house that's also a home meets not just a physical or psychological need but also a spiritual one. In the Bible, God calls his temple "a house of prayer," and heaven is referred to as the Father's house. The Church is supposed to be the great, big, messy, welcoming shelter where all the faithful can be a family, and heaven is that final home where we will find everything that we've lost and be in a place where we truly fit in. There, we will be welcomed among those who love us for who we are. At most times in our lives, we're meant to belong to a parish where we worship in the same place most weeks and have some community with the other parishioners. Some people's vocation leads them to have a home in a monastery or a convent, and others find themselves managing a household with a biological or adoptive family—their path to the heavenly home lies in caring for others in a physical dwelling place. A house, a home, is something we all need and long for with our whole being, not just our bodies.

Christians have a wonderful, solemn obligation to make sure that each of their neighbors has not just a house but a home. Maybe we can't all do the great work the Friendship Room is doing to provide housing and comfortable homes for so many, but we can each do our little part.

How to Shelter the Homeless

- Remember that every time you welcome people into your home, you're allowing them to share a great gift God has given you. Having company for a visit is a blessing. Be thankful for that blessing and be as hospitable as you can.

- In my opinion, every Christian's home ought to be a place where neighbors feel safe going for refuge or if they have a need. How might you do this? What would be your response if a neighbor you didn't know well knocked on your door and asked to use your phone for an emergency? Or if they asked to hide in your house while they waited for the police to come during a domestic violence situation? I think we all should be prepared to do these things. The shelter of our home is a mercy God gave us, not for us alone but so we could share it with our neighbor.

- It's a good idea to patronize charities such as Habitat for Humanity, which builds houses for people who need them, with financial donations and with volunteer work depending on your time and skills. This might be something your parish or school can pull together and have a fundraiser to benefit.

- Prayerfully consider: Are you called to volunteer at a hospitality house such as the Friendship Room? Or if there isn't one in your community, maybe you're being called to form a group of friends and start one. It would take a lot of work, but a home for vulnerable people is always greatly needed.

A house and a home are never given just to the person who lives there. A house and a home are gifts from God that we are supposed to share with anyone who comes to us for help, welcome, comfort, and love. Be thankful for these gifts, and let that thankfulness make you attentive to any way you can spread these blessings to everyone.

Lord Jesus,
You suffered with the homeless
when you had nowhere to lay your head.
Teach me to notice the needs of my brothers
and sisters
who do not have a house or a safe home.
May I honor you, in them, wherever I find
them.
In your most holy name I pray.
Amen.

8.

BEAR WRONGS PATIENTLY

There was a knock at the door and I expected it to be my neighbor again. Our apartment building was built into a little hill, and I had the landlord's permission to use the yard for a vegetable garden. My neighbor's son had helped me weed that garden one day—badly, pulling off the tops of plants instead of getting to the roots, but I'd paid him anyway. We were having an unusually lucky month, and for once I had some money to spare, so I treated him to enough money for a pool pass for the afternoon.

Ever since then, he'd come to the door begging for money at least once a week—and later, his father or mother came by to ask as well. We tried to help when we could. We'd been shown mercy so many times, it would be the worst hypocrisy to not show mercy to a neighbor.

Once, the boy mentioned a sick grandfather they were trying to visit, and I gave gas money. Then he mentioned another sick relative and I helped, and then another. We heard about a tragic house fire in the next town on the news, and that day he came over to tell us that those people were also his relatives and

71

he needed gas money so his father could drive to another hospital. Then, another time, the father came over and said his wife had been fired, and we helped them with a bill. And on it went.

After a short while, though, we caught on that the stories did not add up. The boy likely did not have three grandfathers, unless of course one was a stepgrandfather. The man and his wife both left the house often enough that it looked as though they had jobs. We saw the son happily playing football with friends when he'd said they were going to visit relatives in the burn unit. And anyway, money was very tight for us that month.

Earlier this particular week, however, the man had asked to borrow money from us—not to take it but to borrow until Friday when he'd pay us back. He'd never said anything like that before, so we decided to trust him and handed him twenty dollars.

It was Friday, and so I expected to see my neighbor when I opened the door, though I didn't know whether or not he'd have twenty dollars. Instead, it was my neighbor's son, asking to borrow more. I told him we didn't have any money. But they kept coming back in the weeks that followed. First the son came, then the father, and sometimes his wife. They never paid back the twenty dollars, and they kept asking for more. We kept saying no as politely as we could.

Later that year, another neighbor happened to drop by. She told me about the horrible things the money-seeking neighbor man had been saying about us behind our backs—the crimes and lewd acts he'd accused Michael and me of committing in front of the whole neighborhood. Thankfully, few believed him. They knew he was a liar and a thief. But it was humiliating nonetheless. And there was nothing at all we could do, except stop answering the door, pray for him, and be patient, which I wasn't very good at doing.

God doesn't want anyone to suffer. He especially doesn't want anyone to suffer at the hands of another person. Rather, God wants us to show love for one another at all times. God will redeem all our suffering and make it a source of grace if we bring it to him, but suffering isn't what he wants. Suffering itself is always a bad thing. However, in this fallen world, people use their free will to make bad choices. They hurt and abuse one another. Exactly how this fits into God's plan for creation is ultimately a mystery, but we can be sure of two things: God never wants anyone to hurt anybody else, and people hurt one another anyway. I don't think anybody can get through an entire life without being the victim of another person's sin at some point. It happens to everyone, to some far more often than to others.

Christ suffers with us when we're wronged by others. He knew wrong in his rejection at Nazareth, and in his torture and execution on Calvary. We know that it's not a sin to be a victim of somebody else's sin; if it were, Jesus would be the worst sinner of all. Gazing on the Cross, we realize that a person can be totally without sin and still be abused, even abused until they die. And we can hear Christ's words from the Cross—"Father, forgive them" (Lk 23:34) and "Today you will be with me in Paradise" (Lk 23:43)—and know that even when we're victims of wrong, we can be the ones to help turn the situation to grace by showing mercy.

To bear wrongs patiently does not mean to be a pushover and let someone keep hurting us, as if being a victim of hurt were itself a good thing. Rather, this spiritual Work of Mercy means dealing with situations wherein we are wronged with patience and avoiding making it worse if we can.

We've all heard the serenity prayer, often misattributed to St. Francis: "God, grant me the serenity to accept the things I cannot change, the courage to change the things I can, and the wisdom to know the difference." A wise confessor once told me to change the first line slightly and say, "Grant me the serenity to *acknowledge* the things I cannot change." You don't have to be accepting about things that are genuinely bad. Abortion exists, and we can't change that, and that's horrible. War exists, and we can't change that, and that's terrible. Poverty exists, and Christ said the poor would always be with us, and poverty is awful. We mustn't accept bad things or grow complacent because that's just the way the world is. Instead, we acknowledge that while nothing you or I do on our own will stop these awful things entirely right now, we do whatever we can to help individuals and our cities, towns, and nations make better choices. Then we try to be patient when we can't change what they do. That's what we should seek to do when we bear a wrong patiently: We try to right the wrong, if we can, in a way that is peaceful. And if we can't right the wrong, we at least don't retaliate or make matters worse.

I keep saying that we need to talk about ways in which performing a Work of Mercy in the wrong way can lead to abuse. I believe that trying to bear wrongs patiently in the wrong way can be participating in your own abuse. No one is ever at fault for having been abused; abuse is always the abuser's fault. But you can sometimes make it easier for an abuser to hurt and traumatize you, all while believing you're doing God's will, if you mean to bear a wrong patiently and are actually just being a pushover. That's why it's very important to know what patience is and what it's not.

How to Bear Wrongs Patiently

- Patience does not mean pretending that a wrong done to us is fine. God never expects a person to lie; in fact, lying on purpose is a sin. The first step toward bearing a wrong patiently is being perfectly honest about it. We need to ask ourselves whether the perceived wrong was really a wrong in the first place or if we're the ones being unreasonable. Sometimes the answer is obvious, and sometimes it takes more thinking. Sometimes we might even have to consult another trusted person for advice about whether what we're going through is wrong or not. If we find that we are being unreasonable, we can let go of our frustration and adjust our expectations, and that's a good thing. But if we determine we've really been wronged—if someone else really committed an unjust act that made us suffer—then we have the challenge to handle it with patience as our faith expects of us.

- After we've determined that we were wronged, we have to decide what we can do about it. God doesn't expect any of us to take abuse without standing up for ourselves. There is nothing virtuous about allowing somebody else to hurt us, steal from us, or take advantage of us. The question is how to deal with it in a way that doesn't retaliate or make the situation worse.

- Sometimes the wrong is small, and we're pretty sure it won't happen again—such as a cashier being rude in the checkout or someone screaming at us in traffic. The best course in that case is probably to shrug it off, say a quick prayer for the person, and think about something else. We can practice the Work of Mercy by not harboring anger in our hearts and being careful not to attack anyone else out of stress and frustration. Remember, patience doesn't mean not feeling anger or hurt. It means dealing with the anger and hurt in a way that doesn't add to it, such as through retaliation. If we have to be in such an unpleasant situation, we can at least make sure the hurt stops with us and we don't take our stress out on others.

- Sometimes, however, the wrong is very serious. Sometimes we have to work or live with abusive people who keep hurting us over and over again. And then we have to address those people or find a way to escape, if we can. Remember, God does not want anyone to suffer. There is nothing good or holy about staying in an abusive relationship and taking that pain again and again. If possible, it's much better to talk out our differences and give the person a chance at changing. How to talk about it depends on the situation. In some cases, a letter you've written and revised for clarity will do more good than sitting down to chat; and sometimes the opposite is the case. Think this through carefully and, again, ask a trusted friend or spiritual guide for help determining the best approach.

- In many situations, talking things out is not possible and sometimes it simply won't work. Sometimes it would be dangerous to even try to talk. The only way we can show mercy to people who are truly abusive is to remove ourselves from the situation so they can't commit that sin again. If possible, we might have to change jobs or stop putting ourselves in situations where we're alone with a certain relative or friend. We might even have to cut off someone entirely and not let them be part of our lives, at least for a time.

- Some marriage situations might even require a separation or a divorce for our own safety. A civil divorce is a serious matter, according to our faith, but it is not wrong if it's the only way to protect yourself from abuse, and there should be no shame or stigma associated with that. Divorce and subsequent remarriage without being granted an annulment is something Catholics aren't allowed to do, but just getting a divorce so that an abusive spouse can't come after you and hurt you again is a completely different matter. Staying in a harmful and dangerous marriage is not part of this Work of Mercy.

- However we get free, after we have separated ourselves from an abusive relationship or other serious wrong, we need to take time to heal from what we've suffered. This can often involve seeing a therapist or finding a support group. It's not a sin or a sign of weakness to be traumatized by an abusive situation. Trauma is a real, physical, neurological reaction our bodies have to having been badly hurt and frightened. It's normal, and you will need help getting through it. That's nothing to be ashamed of, and no matter how upset you might feel, it doesn't mean you're not bearing the wrong patiently.

- Sometimes, of course, you can't get away. It's often the case that when a person is living in an abusive situation, they can't immediately find a safe path to escape. Sometimes people are trapped in abusive relationships for years. If that's you, I am so sorry you're trapped right now. Please don't believe it's your fault or that you deserve this. I have been in similar situations, and eventually the door did open to get away to safety and healing. Christ is suffering with you right now, and he will show you the way to safety. Please don't worry too much about whether you're being forgiving enough or patient enough. Keep pouring your suffering out to Christ, and keep looking for support and a way out. I promise you'll find it. I am praying for you.

God doesn't want anyone to suffer, and he especially doesn't want anyone to suffer because of someone else's sin. Unfortunately, in this fallen world, that sometimes happens. When we practice the Work of Mercy of bearing wrongs patiently, we are not allowing people to walk all over us. Rather, we're acting to stop the sin that's been committed if we can, in a way that doesn't retaliate or make the situation worse. And when we can't stop it, we're acting as peacefully as we can in a bad situation until we can find a way out. We are being peacemakers, and as we all know, Christ said that peacemakers are blessed.

Lord Jesus Christ,
Who meekly endured torture and death
to suffer with us, please give me the grace to
    bear wrongs patiently.
Help me to have the serenity to be patient with
    the things I cannot change,
the courage to change what I can without vio-
    lence or retaliation,
and the wisdom to know what is mine to do.
    And what is yours.
I ask this in your most holy name.
Amen.

9.
VISIT THE SICK

It's hard to be alone. This is one of the things people don't always know about chronic illness: it's isolating. Fair-weather friends disappear. You can't necessarily get out of the house when you want to or even when you need to. You may have to cancel appointments and dates at the last minute. You might make a fool of yourself if you try to go out when you're sick—one minute everything is fine, and the next minute you have a bad attack of pain or fatigue and need to lie down, but there's nowhere to lie. If this happens at a friend's house, it's one thing. If it happens out in public—at the mall, the playground, or Sunday Mass—it's quite another.

Some people get angry and offended when someone they know is sick for a long time, especially if they look well sometimes and then very ill at other times, which is often true for those with fibromyalgia. I could be well for weeks and then suddenly sick for months with no explanation and no feasible treatment. Other people's anger at my changes in health was a phenomenon that shocked me at first, because no one had ever explained why people act like that. All I knew was that people I'd considered friends would get angry and tell me I wasn't trying hard enough. They called me a burden and didn't want to talk to me anymore. A priest at a parish we attended went as far as to tell me how shocked other people were by me when I got sick in his church and to angrily yell at Michael about it. We stopped going to that parish. I was so humiliated, I was glad I was too sick to go to church anywhere for a few weeks.

After awhile, I studied and learned the psychological fact that one of the reasons people react angrily to chronic illness is because they are scared. Seeing someone so helpless frightens them because it reminds them of their own mortality and helplessness. We'd all like to believe we're immortal, and nobody likes to think about getting sick. Most of us tell ourselves that we can stay healthy and comfortable if only we take certain precautions. When you're around someone who is chronically ill, you're constantly reminded that this is not true. Chronically ill people are usually taking all kinds of precautions—rest, exercise when we can, medications, supplements, a special diet. And yet we're still sick. We're living proof that even if you do everything right, the human body can break, sometimes for good. And that's scary.

When people are scared, they can channel their helplessness into getting angry without noticing what they're doing. They tell themselves that the chronically ill person must be faking this or just not trying hard enough to get better. And then they lash out, and then they stop being a friend. Of course, some people don't stop being friends because they're angry with you. Some people do it because they just haven't seen you in so long that they forget you exist. Feeling forgotten is one of the most terrible feelings I know.

Shortly after we moved from the terrible apartment I wrote about in an earlier chapter to a rickety rental house on a better street in Steubenville, I had another bad fibromyalgia flare. It started with the fatigue and then weight gain that all happened at once. Part of the weight gain was because I couldn't move to burn any calories, but part of it just seemed to happen no matter what I did. Besides the weight gain, my stomach swelled up into a hard, round bowling ball with gastritis. It hurt to eat. I had to take stomach medication that added to my fatigue and made me put on more weight. My clothes didn't fit, so I was embarrassed to leave the house, which didn't make much of a difference because I was too tired and dizzy to leave the house anyway. My feet went numb and my hands were clumsy. Sometimes it was too much for me to even go up and down stairs, so I stayed in bed. I propped myself up long enough to check my Facebook and my email, and then I would lie back down and drowse most of the day.

Michael had to take care of Rosie full time while I rested. He did all the housework by himself. His only break was after Rosie and I were asleep. He could walk out to the twenty-four-hour eucharistic adoration chapel and pray for a few hours at one o'clock in the morning. Then the other adorer, an older man who lived in a different neighborhood, drove him home, and they chatted for a few minutes on the way.

That was Michael's whole social life during this time. I hadn't had much of a social life to begin with, and now I had none at all. Michael, Rosie, and I went for weeks without company. That hurt. Then one day there was a knock at the door. Michael recognized the visitor as the gentleman from the adoration chapel. "Hi there," he said. "I heard Mary wasn't feeling well, so I brought a relic."

I didn't feel like having anyone in the house because it was so messy. Rosie wasn't very good about picking up her toys at such a young age, and Michael was so busy being the only functioning adult that he couldn't keep up with her. No picking up meant no vacuuming, so the living room was a disaster area. But we let him step in anyway.

The old man was carrying a folded army-green sweater. I thought the sweater must be wrapped around a reliquary of some sort, but as he unrolled it, I saw that there was nothing inside—only the sweater itself, moth-eaten, tattered, and worn. "My son works with the Missionaries of Charity," said the man. "They gave him this sweater that used to belong to Mother Teresa. You can see it's in bad shape, because she always kept the worst things to use for herself. Do you want to put it on and Michael and I can pray with you?"

I did. Mother Teresa's sweater was too small for my swollen arms and couldn't be buttoned, but I wrapped it around my shoulders and put my hands through the sleeves as far as they would go. Now, I've never felt particularly close to St. Teresa of Calcutta. She's not a saint whose memory makes me smile the way some others do. But I loved her just then. I prayed as the old man and Michael prayed. The tight, itchy fabric felt like a hug. And then the man took his sweater back and left, and we were alone again.

I wish I could say there was a miraculous healing from that relic, but there wasn't. I remained sick for quite some time. Gradually, in fits and starts, the flare-up cleared away and left me at my usual low energy and mild discomfort. I learned how to adjust my medicines and vitamin regimen to keep flares from getting so bad the next time. In a real way, nothing changed just at that moment. But in another, I felt much better. I'd been visited by the Communion of Saints—the Church Triumphant in heaven, together with the Church Militant right here on earth.

Most people know what it's like to be sick. Hardly anybody goes through their whole life in perfect health. When we put it that way, it's easier to empathize with someone who is chronically physically or mentally ill—just imagine what it would be like if the sickness went on forever or kept coming back in little bursts with periods of relative good health in between. And we can imagine what it's like to be seriously ill—as sick as you were but worse, more painful, with trips to the hospital or big bottles of medication to cope with, terrible bills to pay, and possibly the fear of death looming.

Put in to perspective like that, it might be even scarier to think about illness. But it's important for us to acknowledge and overcome our fears so we can be of help. Sickness is one of the terrible realities of our fallen world. It's one of those things that really can't be explained, not in a completely adequate way. It's a mystery. God doesn't want anybody to suffer. He wants us to be happy and healthy. He, himself, is life, and he wills us to be alive, and yet here we are suffering and dying. So God comes to dwell with us in our sickness, to suffer with us and transform our suffering into grace. Christ is present in every sick person, sanctifying them. And God is present in everyone who serves the sick, turning suffering into powerful intercession—not because God wills suffering but because if suffering must happen, he's determined to redeem it. It's not good to be sick, but it can become a means of grace, not only for the sick person but also for the people who help them.

We see this grace apparent in so many ways. Think of St. Thérèse of Lisieux on her deathbed proclaiming my favorite aphorism, "*Tout est grace*" or "Everything is grace!" In the midst of horrible physical and emotional suffering, she discovered God suffering with her. And there are many other beautiful saints who went through similar journeys, exercising heroic patience and charity while physically or mentally ill.

Christ could have chosen to redeem the human race in any way he wanted. He could have opened the gates of heaven with one word. But he chose to do it through the path of physical suffering so that everyone who suffers physically would find their own suffering redeemed and given meaning. Everyone who suffers becomes a little Christ, and everyone who attends

the suffering becomes Veronica with her veil, the guard with
his sponge of vinegar, John and Mary attending at the foot of
the Cross.

It's in our own best interest to remember the sick people in
our community and to help them however we can. Our sanc-
tification depends on it. And besides, our sick friends need us.

How to Visit the Sick

- Even though this Work of Mercy is commonly called
  "visit the sick," it's not actually just about physical visits.
  Sometimes the sick person is far away and you can't drop
  everything to go to them. Sometimes they might be in quar-
  antine or some other situation where physical presence isn't
  an option. But you can still fulfill the Work of Mercy by
  writing, calling, texting, and catching up over social media.
  Don't neglect these because they seem less weighty than
  actually visiting in person. Any kind of contact can comfort
  a sick person and help make sure their needs are being met.
- Sick people do need company and to be told they're not
  forgotten. But they also have physical needs that don't go
  away just because they're sick. They might have bills piling
  up, no way to cook dinner for themselves, a house that
  keeps getting messier. Ask what help is needed and try to
  arrange with your community to meet all the needs of your
  sick neighbors.
- At the beginning of a long illness, there's often a flurry of
  activity in the community, arranging a meal train or other
  help for the family. Sometimes nobody even remembers
  to do that, of course, so you should ask around and make
  sure they're taken care of. But either way, after a person's

been sick for a while, there's often a lag where people stop offering help. This is a scary, isolating time. After a friend's sickness has gone on for a few weeks, be sure to check in, ask what help is needed, and at least let them know they're not forgotten.

• You have to consciously remember to check up on your friends who are ill for a long time. I know you don't think you will forget, but it's easy to. Make a note, write it on the calendar, something so you'll have a regular time to call or text them and ask how they're doing and what they need. This really does make a difference in the life of a person suffering from illness.

• When someone you love is sick, fear is a normal reaction. You're afraid for the sick person and what they'll have to suffer. You're afraid they may die and you'll have to go on without them. You're likely also afraid because sickness is a constant reminder of your own mortality, and that's a scary thing to confront. Fear can lead to anger and frustration. It's frustrating to be sick, and it's very frustrating to watch someone struggle with a sickness you can't make go away. But you must not surrender to that frustration and use it as an excuse to attack a sick person. Remember that this isn't their fault. They're not suffering in order to frustrate you, they're just suffering. They deserve patience and compassion. If your anger and frustration get too strong, you might need to seek support from a counselor or therapist to help deal with it in healthy ways, but don't take it out on the sick person or their family.

• People who are sick have families, and those families are also affected by the sickness. If the person is an adult with children, for example, they probably need help with child-care. And even if the regular duties of childcare are covered, the children might really like a day out at the park or the children's museum or the mall with a friend of the family. Offering to take the kids on a trip for the day can be a great way to help the sick grown-up have a day of quiet rest and to ease their mom or dad guilt as well. Sick parents feel terrible when they see that their kids are missing out on fun because of their illness. If the sick person is a child, that child is often (rightfully) getting most of the attention, and the other children can feel neglected, so a treat for them is a good idea. And remember to check up on the sick person's spouse, who probably handles most of their care as well. That's a challenging, stressful situation.

- It's almost never a good idea to badger a sick person with unasked advice about their condition or treatment decisions. There are some exceptions to this. If you suffer from the same condition and the two of you are commiserating, for example, you might mention how you improved with some help they might not have thought of yet. But most of the time, it's just pushy and makes the sick person feel that you're saying they haven't tried hard enough. Don't bother with advice, especially if you're not a medical professional.
- Arrange a giving tree with your parish or school for Advent. Ask a local nursing home or other place where sick and disabled people are cared for long term what gifts the residents want, then organize together to buy them everything on their wish list. And don't stop there. Visit them together to sing carols and get to know them. Make a commitment to come back again, perhaps adapting the place as a regular part of parish life. Organize regular visits and giving.

Sickness is difficult in itself. It's worse when you're sick alone. And watching another person suffer is hard, so it's often the case that we're tempted to abandon sick people. Let us ask God for the gift of compassion and patience, to remain with our sick

neighbors and meet their needs instead of letting them carry
their cross alone.

———————————————

Lord Jesus Christ,
Who endured suffering and helplessness
for my sake and the sake of all the earth,
I thank you!
Teach me to serve you in my neighbors who
    are sick.
Help me not to forget or grow angry with
people who are ill and suffering and helpless
    in our community.
I ask this in your most holy name.
Amen.

10.
FORGIVE OFFENSES

This is a hard one.

I wrote earlier that I had a difficult time with a priest at Franciscan University. Well, now is the time to talk about that.

When I was at Franciscan University, I found a wonderful new family that replaced the close-knit community I'd grown up with in in my hometown. It was a "faith household"—a kind of sorority-like prayer group unique to Franciscan University. I loved those girls like they really were my sisters. We went to Mass together and had weekly parties and Bible studies. When I got married, they were my bridesmaids and sang the household anthem at the wedding. When I started to get sick, at first they were wonderfully supportive—driving me to the doctor and to Church when I was too exhausted to walk, listening when I needed someone to vent to, promising to pray for me when I couldn't be at household meetings. But when I stayed sick, things started to go wrong.

Some of the young women in the household, including the coordinator who was in charge, got impatient. They felt I was being a burden to the other household sisters and that I wasn't trying hard enough or seeing enough doctors to get better. The coordinator got more and more pushy with me, and then she revealed something I'd said in confidence to the rest of the household. I probably could have handled this conflict better myself; indeed, I think the way I rebuked her for doing that was definitely wrong. But I was unused to how people often respond to a chronic illness, so her behavior shocked me and I responded in shock.

I made the mistake of going to the priest in charge of household life for help. I thought that emailing him asking to make the coordinator stop bullying me would make peace, but the result ended up being quite the opposite. First, he sent a series of confusing emails telling me to stay away from household functions. He then ordered me to attend a "conflict resolution" meeting with him and the coordinator where he yelled at me and berated me for talking about my past family struggles (as if my having been abused was too offensive to talk about). He brought me to tears. And then he ordered me to resign from the household without telling anyone why.

The emotional abuse didn't stop there.

After I was officially an "inactive member" of the faith household, about the time I was pregnant with Rosie and still trying to take a few classes to finish my degree, I told some of my former sisters what he'd done and how embarrassing it was. And I wrote him an email describing how his cruelty had hurt me.

He came up with an extraordinarily hurtful way of getting back at me. I have tried and tried to tell myself that the events that followed at Masses were a series of mistakes and not deliberate, but I can't believe that when I look at them all together.

For background, I have a terrible sensitivity to gluten and can't even eat a crumb of it without getting nasty stomach troubles. Also, at this point, Rosie was a new baby. I was regularly walking to Mass on Franciscan University's campus with her in a sling. Thanks to the new-mother hormones still churning through me, my fibromyalgia was in a brief remission, so I could walk a short distance without trouble, and campus was the closest Mass to walk to. I always ended up at the Mass at four o'clock in the afternoon because of Rosie's nap schedule.

During this year, the four o'clock Mass was when they rearranged the front of Christ the King Chapel for their monthly Tridentine liturgy, with the altar pushed toward the back, a makeshift Communion rail made of movable kneelers in the front, and the Franciscan University Schola singing beautiful old hymns accompanied by an organ instead of the usual rambunctious, guitar-driven praise and worship music. The priest who had become my nemesis was the one who officiated the Tridentine liturgy.

A Tridentine liturgy is an easy liturgy for a priest to derail accommodations for gluten sensitivities, since most people only receive the Host and there's not supposed to be multiple chalices.

I told the usher about my gluten intolerance as I came in, and he said there would be a special "celiac chalice" with no Host comingled in the Precious Blood for me to receive from if I came up last. But when I came up and knelt, there was none. The priest asked in a loud whisper if I had "presented myself" beforehand to ask for the chalice, and said that if I couldn't eat the small piece of the Host he offered, there was nothing he could do. I had to walk back with the eyes of the congregation on me. No one in the chapel knew why I'd been turned away from Communion, nor did they know why the other usher called me back to take a gulp from the main chalice—which had a piece of the Host comingled in it and wasn't safe. The schola had finished their hymn by then and the whole church was silent so I felt extra scrutinized.

I assumed this awkward sequence of events had been a coincidence.

So the next time I went to Mass, I asked ahead about accommodations. But once again, there was no celiac chalice when I got to the communion rail by myself at the end of the service. After a nice long pause and whispered conversation (while the whole congregation watched in silence), I finally took a gulp from the main chalice that the other priest held out for me because I was too embarrassed to refuse it. The usher approached me after Mass, confused and apologetic about what could have gone wrong. I was sick from the gluten that evening and the next day.

At the third Tridentine Mass, I was told by the usher that there was a low-gluten Host available for me that the priest would consecrate on a separate paten to keep it safe from cross-contamination. But when I got to the communion rail, I found that the priest had somehow misplaced the low-gluten Host. He stood there looking for it for a long time while I knelt in silence, before the other priest brought me the main chalice again.

Up to that point, I had not had a problem accommodating my sensitivity at a Mass offered by any of the other priests on campus. My other friends with gluten sensitivity who went to Franciscan University had no problem receiving Communion at all that year. Yet somehow, every Mass I went to where this priest was the celebrant ended with my being horribly embarrassed in front of the whole congregation and finally offered a chalice with bits of the Host in it to drink.

The fourth time, I didn't even make it into line for Holy Communion. This wasn't the Sunday they had a Tridentine Mass; it was a Novus Ordo Mass, about which I was relieved. But I started to feel nervous when I saw that the same priest was the celebrant. I was sitting at the front of the crowded church so that I could get to the chalice easily. I was holding baby Rosie, who started to cry and fuss before Holy Communion. The priest simply looked up from the altar and stared at me for a full minute while I tried to quiet her. He stared and stared. He wouldn't continue Mass, no matter how long I looked pleadingly at him and tried to comfort Rosie into silence. He just stood there, with Christ held up in his hands, refusing to say "Behold the Lamb of God" while the congregation waited. Finally I ran out of the chapel, carrying my daughter. And he started up saying Mass again as soon as I was in the foyer.

I stopped going to daily Mass after that. I already had trauma from the spiritual abuse of my childhood. Going to Mass was already painful and often made me cry. Going to Mass was now more frightening than ever, and it still often makes me nervous. I stopped going to daily Masses most of the time, and I dreaded Sunday Mass. For a while I had to get rides to a Byzantine Catholic church across the river from Steubenville, because it was too painful to go to a Latin Rite Mass. It's still not easy for me, to tell you the truth.

That was a horrible, humiliating, abusive thing for a priest to do to anyone. Yet I know God calls me to forgive that priest. This priest hasn't shown any signs that he's sorry or that he wants to change. At this point, I doubt that he'll ever try to make it up to me. But God still calls me to forgive him.

Have I forgiven him? I know that I try to forgive every time I think of him—when I remember, after I finish fuming. And I have come to believe that that's the first step. I have learned from this that forgiveness is not a single event. It is an ongoing process, at least for ordinary human beings—a choice you make not once but as many times as the hurt comes up.

In the gospels, Christ says we are to forgive our brother seventy times seven times (Mt 18:22). Seven, in the Jewish understanding, is a number that stands for infinity. Seven is God's perfect number; the seventh day is the Sabbath, the miraculous day of rest and worship that is outside of time. God himself is also outside of time, in heaven, and when we ask God for forgiveness, he forgives all at once. But for those of us bound by time, I have found it's a different experience.

When we forgive, we become one with Christ on the Cross, praying for his enemies. That's necessary. It's something that we have to do as Christians. But we also have to be careful, because so many things that look like forgiveness are not. Forgiveness is a tricky thing to talk about. In some ways it's not something that we personally do but more of a journey we are taken through by the Holy Spirit. Jesus was perfect and always filled with the Holy Spirit, so I'm sure he forgave all at once on Calvary. We seem to go through it a little differently. For us, forgiveness takes time.

It's helpful to begin talking about forgiveness by pointing to some of the things it's not. Forgiveness does not mean pretending that what the offending person did is fine. Remember what we learned about bearing wrongs patiently: God doesn't want anyone to be hurt, and he doesn't want anyone to lie. Lying is wrong. If someone is asking you to lie to yourself or others about what they did to you, including about how much it hurt, that person is not asking for forgiveness. They're asking you to be dishonest. The only way to really begin to forgive someone is to be perfectly honest about what they did. Asking someone to lie and call it forgiveness is a form of spiritual abuse.

Forgiveness is not "getting over it." It certainly wouldn't be fair of God to demand we get over something before we can forgive because while forgiveness involves a choice, getting over it might be beyond our power. Nobody is in complete control of their emotions, even though we should exercise healthy control over how we vent them. Everyday annoyances and conflicts are one thing, but trauma is quite another. Trauma is real physical injury to the nervous system that can take a lifetime to overcome. Forgiveness can happen after you've gotten over something, but it can also happen in the midst of the messy process of recovering from trauma caused by being harmed.

Forgiveness is not the same as reconciliation. Reconciliation and forgiveness are related but different. Reconciliation means getting back together with someone and restoring your relationship to what it was before. Friends squabble, break up, then apologize and become friends again. A married couple goes through a rough patch, they separate for a time, and then they go to marriage counseling and find a way to work it out and get back together.

Whether reconciliation can happen when you forgive someone depends on what the offense was, how much danger there is of you being hurt again, and whether the offending person is willing to try to change. Remember, God doesn't want anyone to be hurt. Sometimes reconciliation with someone who's hurt you is a necessary part of the process of forgiveness and you can't very well say you've forgiven them if you don't try to reconcile. But sometimes, even though we've forgiven someone, reconciliation isn't possible. Sometimes it would be dangerous and unwise to even try reconciliation, but you can still forgive. You can always forgive.

Forgiveness doesn't mean letting someone off the hook, particularly if you have reason to believe that that person will hurt somebody else. A person who commits a grave wrong may well need to be held accountable for the safety of the community. Anyone asking to be freed from any consequences, especially if they're unrepentant and intend to do the same thing to somebody else, is not asking for forgiveness. They're asking to be allowed to abuse again.

So what is forgiveness, if it's not pretending it didn't happen, "getting over it," reconciliation, or letting someone off the hook? I think that forgiveness is a process that involves a willingness to love someone who has made themselves hard to love. Love is a recognition of the divine image in a human being. When you choose to see God in someone and act to honor God in them, you love. When you really do glimpse that glorious divine image, when you feel God's presence in someone, that's called feeling love or falling in love. When you try to recognize and honor that image in a person who has made it hard for you, that's a choice to forgive. And every time you try to recognize and honor the image of God in a person who has hurt you, even though they've made it so, so difficult, that is part of the lifelong process of forgiveness.

How to Forgive Offenses

- Forgiveness means recognizing and honoring the image of God in somebody. That means doing whatever good you can for them. If a person is a habitual abuser, you honor them by getting away if you can, so that they can't go on sinning against heaven and against you. It might be the only way you can recognize and honor the good in that person, even though it might seem like you're doing the opposite.
- Forgiveness does not mean acting as though the offense never happened, but it might involve declining to gossip about somebody. And this is a tricky subject, because a spiritually abusive person will often claim that any talk of what they did is gossip. The priest told me that sharing my story about him was gossip, but it wasn't. I warned several people about that priest when he was at Franciscan University, and I learned from others that he had the same pattern of verbally abusing them and then being passive-aggressive, so I told even more people for their safety. I was right to do that

because it protected people from him. But I draw the line here: talking in order to help you heal or to protect others from harm is not wrong. But it is wrong to deliberately choose to tell someone what somebody else did *just* to hurt the offender and make them suffer. If that's your motive, that's unforgiving and you should pray for the grace to let go. But don't be afraid to tell your story for other reasons.

- It is never unforgiving to go to authorities to get help against a dangerous person, a person you believe might commit violence against you or somebody else again. That is necessary, and it's helping others, keeping them from harm. Do choose wisely who to talk to, because sometimes people in authority aren't trustworthy, of course. But it's not wrong to get them involved.

- Jesus advises us to "pray for those who persecute you" (Mt 5:44). But I've found that, when you're still smarting from what somebody did to you, it can be retraumatizing to have to think about that person or say their name when you pray. So I think it's perfectly fine to just tell Jesus or Mary that you add that person's conversion and healing to your daily intentions once, and then go on praying as you normally would without repeatedly forcing yourself to think of them.

- Forgiveness involves being honest about what happened to you. It's okay to bring the exact way you feel into prayer. God already knows and doesn't condemn you for it. When you do think of what happened to you, as you experience the pain of a flashback to trauma, tell him everything. Say, "I could just kill that person!" if that's how you feel. And then, as you're able, as you calm down, say, "And I forgive them." Say that even if it doesn't feel true. That's a prayer I've offered many times.

- As you continue your healing journey, you may find yourself angry with God for letting you go through such a terrible situation. God isn't upset with you for feeling that way. He understands that the mysteries of sin and suffering are incomprehensible while we're on earth. He doesn't expect you to understand and accept it without feeling angry. Christ himself asked why he had been abandoned on Calvary. It's okay to feel that you have to forgive God as well as the person who hurt you.

Forgiveness is a beautiful, divine mercy. We act as God our Father does, and as Christ on the Cross did, when we choose to forgive other people. While we are on earth, forgiveness is often a gradual process rather than happening all at once, and that's not wrong. Being able to perform the Work of Mercy of forgiving offenses involves learning what forgiveness is and what it's not so that we can heal and not be hurt in the same way again.

Lord Jesus,
You forgave your enemies on Calvary.
I thank you for forgiving my sins when I come
    to you for mercy.
Please help me to learn what forgiveness
    really is,
and to grant it willingly when I am wronged,
even when it takes a very long time.
I ask this in your most holy name.
Amen.

11.
VISIT THE IMPRISONED/ RANSOM THE CAPTIVE

I grew up believing a certain set of claims were facts. That's how education works, at least in part. Teachers fill your head with nuggets of information. Some of that information is 100 percent accurate. One plus one really does equal two. Some of that information is partly true, correct in certain contexts or with qualifications: yes, Paul Revere did ride at midnight to warn people of an attack by the Redcoats, but he didn't actually yell "The British are coming!" because the American colonists considered themselves "British" at the time. Some of the information is completely false. It's not true that everyone needs six to eleven servings of bread at the bottom of their food pyramid. It's not true that everyone tastes sweet on the tip of the tongue. It's not true that George Washington never told a lie.

Growing up, I was taught that slavery was abolished by Abraham Lincoln at the end of the Civil War and that was the last time that people in America were bought and sold for money. That horrible part of history was over now. I was also taught that people who were in prison were there because they committed a crime, and the way to avoid going to prison was to never commit a crime, and it was as simple as that. We watched educational films, listened to lectures by police officers, and participated in skits to hammer this topic home. Don't commit vandalism. Don't shoplift. Say no to drugs because drug addiction is nothing but a vice. Good people who didn't commit crimes deserved to be free; bad people who committed crimes deserved to suffer and have their freedom taken away. The world was as simple as that.

I learned this view of the world in a Catholic school. Then, later, my family and I left the Catholic school and formed the Catholic community I spoke of earlier. We went to church together at a nice conservative Catholic church with a Communion rail and a beautiful choir. I sang in that choir; I was an alto.

There was a family I didn't know very well, from a different part of Columbus, Ohio, whose mother sang soprano in that choir. They weren't in the homeschool group. The family included two children, which wasn't a lot by the standards of our clique, and we didn't have many of the same circle of friends. Their children were about ten years younger than me, so we didn't play together at all. I knew their little girl only by sight.

Years later, after I'd been in Steubenville a long time, the mother friended me on Facebook. I accepted for good manners' sake; later I friended her daughter as well. We got to chatting about all kinds of things. We were far more alike than I'd imagined. I even found out that we had a distant relative in common on the Irish side of my family. I got to be closer friends with them, through the internet, than I was with the people I'd considered my family back at that church.

One day, in conversation, the daughter mentioned that she was a heroin addict, and I ended up asking her to write a series of articles about her addiction as guest posts on my blog, because it was such a terrible story and so enlightening to me. I hadn't had any idea about the real ways that people can become addicts.

The trail to addiction started for her when she was sexually abused by a babysitter at a very young age, before I'd ever met her. She'd repressed it out of shame and seemed to grow up normally for a time. But as a teenager, all her pain and suffering exploded into post-traumatic stress disorder (PTSD). She was so tormented, she felt she'd do anything to avoid the suffering, so she started binge drinking, which many people with PTSD do to help numb the pain. Mental health care is expensive in the United States and inaccessible for many, but alcohol is cheap. This young woman moved on to other drugs because they calmed the suffering even more—and from then on, she was an addict.

She began working in prostitution to feed her addiction and to buy food for herself, since addicts aren't very employable. Eventually she was kidnapped and trafficked across the state border. Many people who work in prostitution find themselves kidnapped and trafficked, bought and sold, whether they start out as slaves or not. By sheer good luck or an act of Providence my friend was able to escape before it was too late. She went back home and got clean. She had been in recovery for years, relapsing now and then as most addicts do, but fighting every day to stay drug-free.

This is how every addict has to live, wrestling with addiction day to day, knowing full well that they will always be an addict. They will always have to fight off the desire, and there will likely be some relapses, but they keep fighting. This is on top of the horrible situations they were in that made them become addicts in the first place. Many, maybe most, people who struggle with addiction struggled first with another mental illness.

I'd had no idea about any of this. I was humbled by what a strong and compassionate person my friend is. I admired what an attentive mother she is to her children. I was ashamed that I was ever so judgmental about people who struggle with addiction and find themselves breaking the law. I was ashamed that I thought the whole notion of a captive, a prisoner, someone who belongs to somebody else, was a thing of the past.

Meanwhile, I was also learning things from talking to my friends at the Friendship Room and reading about the work they did online. They often welcomed in prostitutes who worked downtown. These women were in the state my friend had been in: addicted to heroin, living from day to day and from injection to injection, trying to stave off withdrawal and make enough money to eat as well. They were often the victims of violence by the men who hired them. Sometimes they would be beaten and robbed or nearly killed instead of paid after they performed whatever the client had asked. They couldn't go to the police for help when this happened, because the police would send them to prison. Many of them had been in and out of prison already. They could go to the hospital for help, but the hospital in Steubenville was only equipped to save their lives in the event of an overdose or other medical emergency. The hospital didn't have a drug rehab program. The women often desperately wanted to go to rehab, but there was no way to send them there.

And some of these women were literally slaves. They had been sold to pimps as teenagers by whomever was supposed to be parenting them when they were too young to say no. Or they had been kidnapped off the street on the way to school one day by people watching them who knew they wouldn't be missed.

Or they had run away from abusive homes and found no one to take them in except pimps. However they got into the hands of their captors, they were forcibly injected with heroin and then they were prisoners. They didn't have anyone who was coming to rescue them. If they ran away, they'd never get far enough, and even if they did, they'd go into withdrawal. If they went to the police for help, the police would arrest them for the crime of prostitution and then they'd go to prison. When they got out of prison with a felony on their record, they'd have even less chance of getting a safe life with housing and a good job than ever. So most of these women would end up in the hands of the pimps again.

The Friendship Room has helped to free some of these women. For others, they've only been able to offer a listening ear, meals, and trips to the hospital. Some of these women have died during the six years the Friendship Room has been open. Heroin-addicted prostitutes don't usually live very long.

My friend is a rare exception, and I'm grateful to God she's alive. I am ashamed that I ever thought that people who are in prison must be there because they "deserve it" and that their suffering is somehow just. I'm ashamed I ever believed that slavery was a thing of the past.

Think about what it means to be free. Nobody is totally free, of course; we all have financial, legal, and physical limits to doing as we please. But try to list all the choices you can make just because you feel like it without having to justify it to anyone. Would you rather sleep with the lights on or off? The window open or closed? Shower before bed or right when you wake up? Hit the snooze button or not? Pray the Divine Office when you get up, say another morning prayer, or make a mental note to pray later? One or two cups of coffee? What do you want in your coffee? What do you want for breakfast? Which blouse or which necktie do you want to wear to work?

What do you want to listen to on your way to work? Are you taking the elevator or the stairs when you get there? And that's just first thing in the morning. Think of every choice you get to make throughout each day.

One of the most basic foundations of our Catholic faith is recognition that we're free to make choices. Some choices don't matter very much and some matter a whole lot, but we are free to make them. We need the teachings of the Church and the grace of the Holy Spirit to make good, moral choices, but in the end, we get to choose right from wrong. If we couldn't exercise our free will, we couldn't ever live a life of virtue. Freedom not only allows us to make the choices that make our lives more comfortable but also it is necessary for the practice of our faith. This is a dreadful responsibility and also a beautiful grace. We, like the angels, get to be free to make choices.

But can you imagine what life would be like if you didn't have choices? If you weren't free? What if somebody kept you in a cage or a cell, decided when you had to have lights on or off, when you had to keep quiet and sleep or pretend to sleep? Imagine eating what was put in front of you on a tray every day, not choosing when to go outside, not choosing what to watch on television or whether to turn the television off, not choosing if you were allowed to go to the library and look at a book that day or ever. What if you couldn't wear a scapular or hold a rosary because those things had been confiscated? What if you didn't know whether you could practice your faith because you didn't know when the prison chaplain was coming or whether he was coming at all?

There are two names for this Work of Mercy: visit the imprisoned and ransom the captive. This points to two different groups of people: those who are imprisoned by their government, some of whom are guilty of crimes and some who aren't; and people who are captives for other reasons, such as human trafficking. Both of these people have been denied freedom. In this Work of Mercy, Jesus calls us to remember everyone who is not free, whether or not we think they deserve to be free, whether it's criminals or civil authorities who have taken away their freedom.

Yes, it's true that sometimes people have to be locked away somewhere so that they won't hurt anyone. But our faith values freedom so much that we all ought to think of that as a last resort in an emergency, not as a convenient place to put anyone who commits a crime however nonviolent. Rehabilitating people so that they can be free is always the better choice.

And yes, it's true that people who have been violent or hurt others deserve to be punished. All have sinned, and everyone deserves to be punished. But that's the thing about mercy. Mercy never uses the word *deserve*. Mercy looks at the intrinsic value of human beings and honors what God created, even when that person has behaved in a way that merits a punishment. Mercy means we don't have a right to discriminate between people in prison who appear to deserve it and people in prison who were falsely accused. They're all God's children. We should fight for freedom for the wrongly imprisoned. But we also have to visit and care for the needs of people in prison who are guilty of crimes, because every human being is worth caring for.

Christ suffered with victims of human trafficking when he was sold to his enemies by Judas. And he suffered with those who were imprisoned by the government when he was kept in chains by the local Jewish leaders and then tried and executed by the Romans. When we minister to victims of human trafficking and people in prison, we are serving Christ in his Passion.

How to Visit the Imprisoned and Ransom the Captive

- There is really no such thing as a "deserving person," when we talk about mercy. When you look at someone in prison, never think, "Serves them right." Instead, try to empathize. Also remember that so many people end up prisoners due to misfortune and not wickedness. Especially remember this in light of immigration issues and issues that disproportionately affect poor people and people of color. Hunger can lead a person to shoplift. Being abused as a child can lead a teenager to be violent. Maybe you think you'd never steal, assault someone, or turn to drugs. But imagine what life would be like if you suffered from severe trauma like my friend did, if you were so poor you couldn't afford to eat, or if you had no safe place to go. What happened to the people who are in prison could happen to you.
- The Innocence Project is a nonprofit organization that helps to exonerate wrongfully convicted people through DNA testing. This evidence might have been ignored or might not have been available to prisoners when they were tried. Donating money to the efforts of this organization is a great way to free people suffering wrongful imprisonment. You can donate to them yourself, and you can also organize a fundraiser through your parish, community, or school.
- You can also raise money for charities such as the Nomi Network, which work to free trafficked and enslaved people and provide them with safe housing and work training so they don't get caught up in trafficking again.

- Right now, most people who enter the United States as immigrants at the southern border are immediately treated like criminals even if they're not dangerous and even if they come into the country without breaking immigration laws. They are put in inhumane detention centers for a very long time, if no one can pay their bond, and the bond is often set very high to filter out the immigrants who might be poor. You can assist them by donating to organizations that pay bond for immigrants and set them up in housing with food to eat and English lessons until their asylum hearing and by donating to organizations that get the immigrants legal assistance. Two of my favorite charities for this Work of Mercy are the Refugee and Immigrant Center for Education and Legal Services (RAICES) and Immigrant Families Together. The latter in particular just has one enormous GoFundMe for all of their expenses, and every one of the people who work for them is a volunteer. All of your money will go right to the immigrants who need help.

- Educate yourself about the plight of trafficking victims and about what people go through in prisons and jails whether they're guilty or not. Everyone has notions and prejudices about people in prison and people who become prostitutes; make sure that your impressions are correct. That way, when you are talking with your friends and the people in your community, you'll be able to help them understand. The better educated our society is, the better chance we have of helping people instead of making their situation worse.

- See if there's a ministry in your parish for visiting prisoners, tutoring them in reading, or sending them letters and care packages. That's a way to help them and also to build your own empathy.

- Make your voice heard in your politics. I'm not going to tell you what political party to vote for. If you're an American, both major political parties are pretty horrible. But remember that politicians work for you. Don't miss the opportunity to write to your representative, sign petitions, participate in peaceful protests and other things that can sway legislators to reform the laws so that prisoners are treated humanely, so that people can get the mental health and financial help they need so they don't commit crimes in the first place, and so that those who have committed nonviolent offenses don't get incarcerated or not for very long. Also look into the laws surrounding prostitution and human trafficking where you are and make your voice heard about them as well.

- If there's a Catholic Worker House or another hospitality house such as the Friendship Room in your city, they often minister to people trapped in modern-day slavery. Sometimes you can help them get free. In any case, you can help make their lives a little easier.

Freedom is a gift from God and a necessary one if we're going to practice Christianity. Our faith requires us to do what we can to set captives free and to help ease their suffering even when we can't. This is a wonderful way to thank God for our own freedom and never take it for granted again.

Lord Jesus,
You suffered trafficking at the hands of
    Judas Iscariot
and imprisonment by your own people and the
    Roman occupiers.
Thank you for being present with those who
    are denied their freedom.

Teach me to serve you in people who are
    imprisoned and enslaved.
I ask this in your most holy name.
Amen.

12.
COMFORT
THE AFFLICTED

I was having a hard time, but I can't remember what I was so upset about. Maybe I was making a fuss over nothing, or maybe I was overwhelmed by something serious. I've had plenty of both kinds of moments in my life. Perhaps I was just exhausted.

At this point, you can probably see that being poor and chronically ill, raising a child in a place where you don't have many friends or family nearby, and recovering from spiritual abuse is both physically and emotionally draining. I still don't feel I've done justice to just how stressful it is. Not knowing how you're going to live from month to month is terrifying, and that terror can wear people down over time no matter how brave they are. And being poor also robs people of any number of good ways to cope.

I don't know that I was ever brave, but I know that I was badly worn down. I was sad and afraid all the time, and exhausted from bearing that sadness and fear. I felt guilty for raising my daughter in poverty when I wanted to do so much better for her. And I couldn't do anything with that exhaustion, fear, and sadness. I couldn't go on vacation or head to the mall for shop-ping therapy. I couldn't even go out to dinner and treat myself to a rich dessert. One of the only outlets I had was crying alone in my room, or maybe not even crying, at least not physically, but moping alone in my room. I'd refer to it as taking a nap, but I wasn't asleep.

That's where I was, lying in my bed and crying either inwardly or outwardly, when my daughter toddled in. I don't think she was older than two. She was in her usual uniform of a pink cloth diaper and a T-shirt. Her eyes were wide with concern. I tried to hide my upset, as grown-ups do, but Rosie was too smart for that. "What's de matter?" she wanted to know.

I'm not sure what I said. Something that grown-ups always say, downplaying the situation. "Oh, I'm feeling a little sick right now." Something like that. Rosie's answer was perfect: "I can care for you!" She climbed into my bed and gave me a long hug.

"Oh, thank you! I'm very glad about what a caring person you are," I told her. "Now, what's de matter?" Rosie demanded. "I'm just feeling a little sick," I fibbed. "I'll be okay."

Rosie toddled out of the room. She came back in with a plate containing one sticky gluten-free pancake left over from breakfast. "I brought you a pancake to cheer you up!" she said. "Oh, thank you," I said. "But I don't have a very big appetite just now." "Dis is a big pancake to give you a big appletite," insisted Rosie. "We'll split it." And we did. We sat up in bed together, each munching on half a pancake. And I did feel much better.

Rosie did that again many times when she was small—say-ing "I can care for you" with an earnest hug when I looked upset, followed by bringing me something to cheer me up. And she expected the same from me. Sometimes I'd catch her doing a pratfall and asking "Care for me!" when she was upset or hurt. I always did, by giving her a hug and spending time or having a snack with her. She meant "Comfort me," but either way she was on to something. Rosie recognized the hug and the attention as a kind of care, as necessary as food. And she was quite right about that.

When a person in the community is suffering, that makes a demand on Christians. We ought to find out why and meet their needs in any way we can. But beyond that—and often prior to that, as Rosie demonstrated—we ought to simply be present to them. A person who is suffering might well need to be reasoned with. They might need instruction or admonishment. They often need material help. But they also need company, someone to listen to them, someone to assure them of their presence—sometimes a hug. They need this as much as they need anything else, but in our society I think it can be the hardest form of care to come by.

I would guess that most everyone can remember one time in their lives when a bad thing got much worse because they felt alone with no one to comfort them. I think most everyone also remembers a time when things were difficult but felt easier because somebody was there to listen, to commiserate, to sympathize, to offer a hug. Christ certainly knows what this is like. Think of his sorrow in Gethsemane, when none of his apostles would stay awake with him.

Staying awake to comfort the suffering is a sacred way of serving God, because it is a way of caring for people. Feeling affirmed and accompanied is as necessary for mental health as food, water, clothing, and shelter are for physical health. It's not something we can live without.

In a world so full of pain, it's possible to go into a sort of panicked fluster and forget how to comfort people. We become so focused on action and results that we're frustrated by anything that simply requires presence. It's comparatively easy to hand somebody a sandwich for their hunger, or a coat for their chills, or even to help them with their homework and read flash cards to them. Just to be present to them, not performing a set task but being there to comfort someone in a difficult time, is so much harder. But it's necessary.

When someone is suffering, what is your response? Do you want to get away because it's awkward and embarrassing? Do you try to push a solution onto somebody's problems at once, without stopping to empathize and understand first and perhaps not realize you're acting to soothe your own discomfort and not that person's pain? Do you get angry and lecture the person, call them selfish, remind them that other people have suffered in their lives too, as if pain were about bragging rights and who gets to win?

Next time, stop. When another person's suffering feels embarrassing, think how embarrassed they must be. When it makes you uncomfortable, think about how much more uncomfortable they are. When you feel the urge to one-up them about somebody else's problems, stop. This person, right now, has these problems and they hurt, no matter what else is happening in the world. This person needs you to care for them. This is Christ appealing to you to perform a Work of Mercy.

How to Comfort the Afflicted

- How, exactly, you can perform this Work of Mercy depends on your relationship to the suffering person. Perhaps you're far away when you hear of their misfortune, and all you can do is send a sympathy card, a heartfelt letter, or a care package. Don't neglect to do that, according to your means. Think about what the person likes and choose a gift or a card that shows some thought instead of something chosen at random. It doesn't have to be expensive to make a person feel loved, but it does have to look intentional.

- It could also be that you're physically near people but the suffering person doesn't feel safe sharing in detail or wants to be alone. It's a good idea to ask the person who is suffering, "Would you like me to stay with you or do you need space?" and then to not get offended no matter what the answer is. Sometimes the answer is that they need space at first and want to talk later, so you should be ready to do a little of both. If someone is going through a long-term struggle such as depression or grief from the loss of a loved one, they might need long stretches of alone time and also company now and then, so ask after them often.

- Such a person might also believe that they're being a burden and not worthy of being comforted by others, so make sure they know that you don't mind and would like to help as often as they need to hear it. Let them know you're available if they do want to talk, be patient if they can't talk at first, and really listen when they eventually do—however long that happens to take.

- Try to empathize with the suffering person; try to imagine what you would feel like in their shoes. But don't be dishonest with yourself or them either. Don't say "I understand!" if you don't. It's okay to say something like "I can't imagine what you're going through, but I'm so sorry and I want to help." Put it in your own words so it sounds genuine, but saying something like that is fine.

- After you've listened, offer to help if you can, even if the only help you can give is being present to comfort that person the next time they need it. But if there's something else you can do—another Work of Mercy such as bringing them a meal or looking after their children while they're sick—offer that too, or refer them to someone who can help if you're not able.

- Obviously, sometimes a suffering person needs special help you can't provide. It's good to suggest that your friend with a mental health struggle see a therapist, for example. But remember that a person who struggles with their mental health can't get well through therapy alone. Everyone needs a community of family and friends for good mental health. So don't shy away from them or insist they don't tell you how they feel just because they have a mental illness. You wouldn't shun your friend with a broken leg because you're not an orthopedic surgeon, would you?

Humans are not just bodies; we have minds and hearts that need care as much as our bodies do. It's important to just be available to a person who is suffering, not necessarily meeting any physical needs but comforting them emotionally. When you do this, you are comforting Christ. You are being a disciple who stayed awake with the Lord in Gethsemane. We *can* care for one another, as Rosie realized. And this is a wondrous grace.

Lord Jesus Christ,
You begged your disciples to stay awake with
    you,
please give me the grace to comfort my neigh-
    bors who are suffering.
Help me to be present and attentive to them
rather than pushing you who are present in
    their affliction away.

I ask this in your most holy name.
Amen.

13.
BURY THE DEAD

Rosie and I like to play in the cemetery. Does that sound strange to you? There's not a terribly large amount of natural spaces in Steubenville. There isn't much that's pretty to look at in town, especially not within walking distance of our neighborhood. It's mostly gray and unpleasant. But behind the supermarket near our house, there happens to be a cemetery.

Some of the graves in this cemetery are more than two hundred years old. There are veterans of the Revolutionary War buried there, as well as many veterans of the Civil War. The trees there are breathtaking—venerable old trees. There are forests and streams to enjoy and walking paths that run by them. This cemetery is nicer than the park, quieter and easier to pray in than a church. And it's open from dawn 'til dusk with no entry fee. I love it there. When we move out of Steubenville, it will be one of the very few places I'll miss.

When Rosie was a baby, I would push her up and down the cemetery roads in the stroller. If we had any money for it, we might go to the nearby Chinese restaurant and get rice for a picnic on one of the park benches there. If all we had was the food stamp card to spend, I would buy some fruit and gluten-free granola bars at the grocery store to eat there. When she got a little older, we used the graveyard for our homeschooling nature studies. We talked about the names of different kinds of trees and wildflowers. I taught her what was poisonous and what wasn't. We watched birds, deer, and squirrels under the trees. We looked at headstones.

Rosie was a bit delayed in learning to read. Sometimes I'd make her sound out people's names, but usually she had me read them to her and tell her how long ago the person had lived and how long their life had been. We noted all the "husband" and "wife" graves, the family plots all organized together, and the markers that showed where one family plot ended and another began. Rosie was full of questions about graves. How did a person make sure that they'd be buried next to a loved one? Could you be buried next to anybody you wanted?

Once we saw a headstone that had fallen over. Rosie bent to inspect the stone slab at the bottom of where the headstone had been. "Is that his coffin?" she asked, and I explained about bodies being buried six feet under. I noted the graves of married couples, especially those where the death dates were far apart. Some people died within a year of one another, and some had very different journeys. I wondered what it must have been like to lose a spouse and have to go on for a decade or more without them, trusting that your spouse was waiting in heaven. There was even the grave of a man who had married twice, with one wife beside him and then the other next to them, and I thought about the parable of the woman with seven husbands. I saw graves marked with "grandfather" and "grandmother," and I prayed for my own grandparents, three of whom are already dead and buried far away.

I prayed for all the dead, in this cemetery and elsewhere, especially those who had no one to pray for them. And I believe that the dead in that cemetery who are already at rest see me praying and pray for me in return. I often shuddered at the graves of infants—babies who lived just a month or only a year. Those are less frequent in modern times, for which we should be thankful. Vaccination and modern sanitation prevent a world of horror. Some graves were marked with the names of several children, born in different years and then all wiped out at the same time. I couldn't imagine going on after suffering a loss like that, but many parents have.

Of course, sometimes babies still die. Molly, who helped found the Friendship Room, lost a baby. Little Oliver has a grave. I have other friends who have lost babies. They go to the cemetery and decorate the graves with balloons and rainbow flowers on their birthdays or their due dates, if they died in the womb. I prayed for their consolation.

Time and again, Rosie and I saw the words "perpetual care" carved into stones. I actually thought that that was some kind of sentiment at first, similar to "Gone but not forgotten," but eventually I realized that it wasn't. It was the indication that this person's family had paid ahead for the cemetery caretaker to care for the grave site. Some of the headstones in the cemetery were original. But the suspiciously clean and new-looking ones with the very old dates were replacements, provided by the cemetery because of the perpetual care fund.

The people were long dead. Their bodies in the old-fashioned pine boxes were probably completely returned to the soil by now—dust to dust, as is right and proper. The trees growing around the graves must have been saplings when they were planted, but now they were towering thick trunks that shaded the whole cemetery plot. Nature being what it is, some of the material that the trees use to nourish themselves through the roots probably came from the decaying bodies under the soil. The trees are all that's left of the bodies of the people buried here. But their names are not forgotten, because the cemetery kept the stones clean and readable and replaced them when it was necessary.

Without that work and the money that paid for it, the cemetery couldn't be maintained as a place to hike and think about the living and the dead. We'd never remember the people who died a century ago. We wouldn't think about them. I wouldn't have a place to walk with Rosie and meditate on death. I wouldn't have been reminded to pray for the souls of those who are long gone. I wouldn't be reminded so often about my beloved grandparents, and pray for them, and tell Rosie stories about what they were like. Mothers and fathers who lost children wouldn't have a place to go and put down balloons and colorful flowers and remember them. We wouldn't speak so often about death and remember that we were dust and pray.

One day, we hiked past a very large headstone, almost as tall as I am. Carved into the stone was a tacky-looking representation of the risen Christ. "It's Jesus!" said Rosie. "So that's where he's buried." I laughed without thinking and reminded Rosie that Christ is risen from the dead.

But I also took it seriously, because she'd told me a powerful truth. Jesus is buried in that particular grave, and in the grave next to it. He is buried in every grave in that cemetery and in every burial place on Earth, from the prehistoric burial grounds to the mausoleums that were just built yesterday. Because Christ comes to us in human beings. Humans are tabernacles of Christ. When Christ died on Calvary and was buried, he died our death and was buried in our graves. He died and was buried in all of us.

Every time you do something physically to honor a deceased person—paying for a burial, helping to maintain a grave site, going to a wake—you are performing the Work of Mercy to bury the dead. When we perform this Work of Mercy, we are helping to honor the dead person's body one last time. One last time, we get to pay homage to Christ who became a man with needs and feelings and vulnerabilities, for our sake. One last time, we get to perform a service for the bodily, physically vulnerable parts of human beings. After we commit their bodies to the ground, all that's left is to pray for their souls.

But when we perform the Work of Mercy to bury the dead, we are also performing a Work of Mercy for the whole community. Everyone who walks past that grave will have the opportunity to remember, meditate, and pray, because of what we did. We comfort grieving people. We provide a place to pray and reflect. We even honor nature.

We honor Christ not only in his death and burial but at Gethsemane and every other place and time that he went off to find a quiet place to pray. This final corporal Work of Mercy is a Work of Mercy for the whole life and an invitation to a wonderful grace.

How to Bury the Dead

- Every person's body is a kind of relic. Every person's body points toward the resurrection of the dead. We should be reverent with the bodies of the dead and never show them disrespect. But that doesn't mean we should always be sad and act depressed around them. It's okay to go for a walk or jog in the cemetery just to enjoy the trees and fresh air, or to have a snack on a park bench. But don't be rowdy, loud, or disrespectful. It's not the same as going to church, but it's not a noisy place either.
- Schedule a day to go to your family's plot in the cemetery, if you have one. Pull weeds, clean the gravestone, and plant flowers. Take a longer time than you think you'll need, and

bring the children along. This is a Work of Mercy your family can do together, and you might find yourself talking and sharing stories of the deceased in order to pass along their memory.

- If you're visiting a cemetery and see some graves that don't look well kept, pull up the weeds around them and say a prayer for that person.
- If the loved one of someone in your community has died, don't neglect to visit the calling hours and the funeral. Just being there is a way to show honor to the dead—and to comfort your friend as well.
- Organizations such as Children's Burial Assistance, the TEARS Foundation, and Final Farewell help grieving parents pay for the unexpected expense of burying a child. Many people who go through the tragedy of losing a son or daughter don't have the money for a funeral and burial. Having to fundraise for this expense can be an added trauma, and a donation to these organizations will spare a parent that suffering.

Bury the dead is the final corporal Work of Mercy. It's the last way we show respect for a human body, the final respect we pay before we see that body again at the resurrection of the dead. Every time we honor the grave of a deceased person, we're honoring Christ in his burial and showing faith in his resurrection. But we're also honoring our whole community, our own bodies, and the natural world in which we dwell.

Lord Jesus,
you came to die so that we might live
and so that no one ever die alone.
For this grace, I thank you.
Please help me not to neglect honoring the
    dead
with this final corporal Work of Mercy.
I ask this in your most holy name.
Amen!

14.
PRAY FOR THE LIVING AND THE DEAD

I met a man and woman riding on the bus. I'd been to the library for Story Time with Rosie, and we were on the bus heading back home. They were sitting in the seat behind us. The man and woman admired Rosie and told us they had ten children of their own, though the oldest was grown up now and a missionary. The youngest was just a little older than Rosie was. They told me, as if it was the most normal thing in the world, that they had come from Texas because they lost their jobs there and felt as though they needed a change. So they asked God where he wanted them to move. God had apparently directed them here, and they obeyed. They said they were always doing things like that, and they told us that the moment they'd gotten to Steubenville, all eleven of them had had to pawn their coats and boots to get money to buy food. When they found out I was Catholic, the couple invited me over to their house to pray.

The house was just a few blocks from the rickety rental house Michael and I were living in. It was on a much scruffier block than our house, was smaller than ours, and had no real yard. Their children were practically bursting out of the house at the seams like an illustration for the poem about the old woman who lived in a shoe. All the boys were in long pants and all the girls in long skirts and sweatshirts even though it was late spring, because they were from Texas and they were freezing.

We had supper at a table that ran the length of the tiny dining room. The father said, "Let's hear it for God!" and the children cheered. He said, "And the devil?" and the children booed. This was their normal evening routing. We ate, not very heartily because there was precious little food. Then we moved into the tiny living room, sang hymns, and prayed the Rosary. Several of this family's neighbors had come over to pray as well. After we prayed, they went around the room talking about their week and asking for advice. The family huddled around those neighbors and prayed over them.

The community I grew up in prayed the Rosary together and that was wonderful. But I didn't like to think about my old community. Sometimes, praying in a group like that makes me nervous and triggered. But somehow, in that family, it felt good. I even let them pray over me.

I was invited back, and I went back. I went every Tuesday night for a while. The children loved Rosie and would push her up and down the block in a wagon after we prayed. Sometimes I would see the family on the bus. Sometimes I'd see them driving an absurdly banged-up old sixteen-passenger van through the neighborhood. Once they offered me a ride, and I sat in the back among an enormous pile of empty water jugs that I didn't ask questions about.

On one of my trips to the family's house to pray, I went upstairs to use the bathroom. There was a jug of water from the grocery store beside the sink, which I didn't think about at first. But then I went to flush the toilet and it made a funny noise. And then I went to wash my hands and found there was no water coming out of the tap. I leaned across the minuscule shoebox of a bathroom to turn on the shower and rinse my hands, but the shower didn't work either.

I realized that these people were poorer than I was, with far more children to spread the money between. They'd had their water shut off, just as Michael and I had almost had happen so many times. The price of water was so high that paying the fee and the fines to get it turned back on was out of the question. So they spent some of their food stamp money on bottles of water. I assume they were filling those jugs of water in the van somewhere as well. There's a pump that the baseball players use to fill their water bottles by the baseball diamonds in the park nearby. I wondered if they were using that.

As the summer went on, they mostly ate and served me the vegetables—stewed tomatoes, big bowls of green beans—they grew in a spot in a community garden in a different part of the neighborhood. I wished I could bring them more food, but this was during a bad summer for Michael and me as well. We didn't have anything.

The family never looked discouraged, though. They always seemed happy. They always sang hymns and prayed with me. And then the father would say, "Don't send her home empty-handed!" and the mother would give me some fresh tomatoes to take home.

Eventually they left or got kicked out of that house. Several times a year I kept seeing them around town, and they'd smile happily and tell me what a mess they were in this time. Once, they lost their van and had to take the whole eleven-person family on the bus until someone gave them a new one. Once, they got a bad deal on a derelict house that was rent-to-own even for people with bad credit. Once, I got to meet their brand-new baby, baby number eleven. I remembered the mother talking about how much she liked midwives, and I privately wondered if they'd ended up with the same fake midwife who'd duped me. Once, they got raided by the police—not social services but the police. Someone had noticed that the children looked sickly, so instead of trying to help or find out what the problem was, they called the police. The community could have helped if they'd understood, but instead they didn't bother to understand and called the cops.

Thankfully the police realized there wasn't a crime here, just hunger. Social services got involved to work with the parents and help them. The next time I saw the family they looked in much better health. Stories where the police get involved when only poverty is to blame don't often have a happy ending like that, and I'm grateful that this one does.

Shortly after this, I found a GoFundMe on the internet raising money for this family to get new housing. I recognized their picture and name. That month I had a little money, so I chipped in, and I prayed that others would chip in. The next time I saw them, they were even happier than usual. They were walking in the opposite direction I was, down a sidewalk on a noisy, busy street, but they stopped right there to greet me.

"Can we pray?" they said excitedly, shouting a little to be heard over the cars. "It just feels like we should!" I shouted yes and bowed my head, and they put their hands on my shoulders. "Are you open to hear a Word from the Lord?" shouted the mother.

People who offer to give you a Word from the Lord are a dime a dozen in Steubenville. Many of them are self-serving and blame the Lord for any impulse to do as they please. I had been abused in the name of the Lord from the time I was a little girl, in that wonderful homeschooling community that was also so terribly abusive. I usually say no to Words from the Lord, but this time I said yes.

"Precious daughter," they said, or I guess the Lord said through them, "I have not forgotten you." I had never told anyone that I felt forgotten. "I see the silent tears you cry at night. Stop."

Sometimes I did cry myself to sleep at night. Other times I wished I could find an outlet for my worry and trauma in tears, but I just cried inwardly.

"First the root grows out of the seed, then the first leaves appear, and everyone sees the tree, but *I* see the root," they, or God, finished. Those words have haunted me ever since.

God sees the root. God saw everything I had been through in Steubenville and knew how to put it to use. And he has. Working as a professional blogger for Patheos Catholic now, I live on gratuities from patrons, and it's still touch-and-go, but we've been off food stamps for a while now. We're going to have a car before long, and we're slowly working our way out of this miserable hole of poverty. Now I get to use what I've learned. Now I write about the sufferings that poor people, sick people, captive people, and traumatized people face, among other things. Now I get to write about spiritual abuse and help people heal and tell their stories. Now, instead of needing to be rescued with water and salad from the Friendship Room volunteers, we bring them groceries at least once a month, and I buy them the food I used to daydream about when we had next to nothing. I have learned so much about what it's like to be poor, sick, and lonely that I have something to tell other people, so that we as Christians can help one another. God didn't want me abused, but he has used my journey to help me tell other people about what it's like so it's not so hard and isolating for them. I couldn't have done that before.

At the time, standing on the side of that noisy highway with two strange people praying over me, I couldn't see that any of that would ever happen. I felt trapped, poor, unemployed, alone, in a scary part of town, with no way out.

God needed a way to get through to me and he chose poor people. He usually does. Christ chose to come to us as a poor man, the son of a poor woman, the foster son of a poor laborer. He still comes through people who are poor and helpless, if only we learn to we meet him there.

And God chose prayer. He chose two poor people offering to pray over me and then waited for me to say yes. Through that, God told me something that would later come true.

Prayer was the way he got through to me. Prayer is always the way he gets through. Prayer is something that brings us into the life of the Holy Trinity.

It's impossible to explain exactly what the Holy Trinity is. All of our words fall short. But the Trinity is like, among other things, an eternal waterfall of love pouring out from the Father into the Son, and from the Son back to the Father, each giving his whole self to the other. And the movement of that love is a person known as the Holy Spirit. The Holy Trinity is something like that.

The Holy Trinity is eternally pouring out, eternally loving, and eternally breathing that love and mercy who is the Holy Ghost. That movement never had a beginning and never comes to an end. When Jesus, here on earth, prayed to the Father—that was a glimpse into the movement of the Trinity.

The Trinity is God eternally praying to God, Light from Light, True God from True God. And human beings are made in the image and likeness of that perpetual flowing.

One of the ways in which we are images of God is that we pray. We enter into the movement of the Trinity when we do what the Trinity does and love the Trinity. God is already present everywhere. But in a sense, prayer is God picking up a human being and holding them in the middle of the Trinity so that all this life-giving love flows through them like a prism.

In the first chapter of this book, I told you that feeding the hungry helps complete the Father's act of creation, by getting the food he created into the stomachs of the people who need it to live. All the Works of Mercy do about that same thing: they are ways in which we help God complete creation by getting the food and water, shelter and dignity, knowledge and righteousness God created to the people who need these graces. Whenever we perform a Work of Mercy, we are stumbling into God's work, into the movement of the Trinity.

This final spiritual Work of Mercy, to pray for the living and the dead, is an especially lovely way of completing God's creation. When a soul goes to heaven, that's the completion of a work that began when God the Father created the heavens and the earth, that was purchased and sealed when God the Son submitted himself to sacrifice on Calvary, that was continued when God the Holy Ghost descended to the apostles and through them, to us. St. Athanasius said, "God became man so that man might become God," and "becoming God," getting drawn up forever into the glorious movement of the Holy Trinity, is what heaven is.

A Christian is always being drawn up into that divine movement, by the grace of God, whenever they choose to try to follow God. We are certainly drawn up whenever we perform a Work of Mercy. Particularly when we pray, we are making a little visit to heaven. When we intercede for another human being, living or dead, we're doing what God does—we're taking that soul and lifting them up into the life of Holy Trinity; we're lifting that soul to heaven.

Sometimes people have a strange way of looking at prayer. They seem to think that prayer and the other Works of Mercy are somehow opposed. You have no doubt seen some Catholics scoff at other Catholics who are very hands-on working with the poor, caring for the environment, going to protest marches for a just cause; they claim those are "social justice warriors" and not "real Catholics." But you'll also find people very caught up in doing good work for others who scoff at prayer and think it's a lazy substitute for the other Works of Mercy. I don't see it that way at all, and I'm sure the Church doesn't either.

Intercession is one of the Works of Mercy. It's not at all a lazy thing; it's work, a real discipline, even a battle sometimes. Our prayer should inspire us to action to help those we're praying for, as the Holy Father, Pope Francis, said recently, "You pray for the hungry. Then you feed them. That's how prayer works."

Prayer for others should constantly challenge and remind us of how we can better serve them. But prayer itself also helps. Somehow, by the mercy of God, through the working of the Holy Spirit, prayer softens hearts. It speeds healing. It encourages. It can even work as a catalyst for desperately needed social change. No one is sure how prayer works, but it does. Rather than an excuse for inaction, prayer should inform, nourish, and sustain our action. We should pray to be inspired with how to help our neighbor. We should pray for our neighbor as we help. And we should pray for all the ways that God can help our neighbor when we cannot. All of those are necessary.

Praying for somebody can be abusive if it's done as a substitute for loving them in all the ways they need rather than as one way of loving them. Think of someone who's capable of feeding a hungry beggar outside the church door but opts to only pray for that beggar to get his act together instead. Or think of an abusive parent who goes to daily Mass to pray for their children but neglects the children's physical and emotional well-being.

There's also a certain type of performative prayer—prayer said out loud in inappropriate contexts with manipulative motives—that can be abusive. Think about a situation where someone is standing outside an abortion clinic praying loudly, not inviting pregnant women to make a different choice or offering them any help but shouting prayers for their repentance to humiliate them. It's not necessarily wrong to pray at an abortion clinic, but I as I mentioned earlier, I've often witnessed people praying so loudly that sidewalk counselors can't be heard when they gently offer help. And I've also seen situations where an abusive person announces that they're praying for someone in a way calculated to embarrass or annoy them. When prayer is used as a substitute for action or a tool for manipulation, it's ugly and destructive. But when we pray in love and not in a manipulative way, and as long as we're not neglecting to do anything else we ought to do for that person, we can help others in countless ways.

HOW TO PRAY FOR THE LIVING AND THE DEAD

- The Church has many prayers that are meant to be prayed daily, to help our lives be centered around prayer. The Rosary is one of them that many people know. It's a beautiful prayer, a prayer that leads us to meditate on the Gospel. I have, however, met many people who are victims of spiritual trauma, who find they can't pray the Rosary because it brings back horrible memories. I go through times when it hurts too much to pray a Rosary. If you're one of those people, please don't feel guilty. It's not your fault. There are other forms of prayer that work just as well. Find one that doesn't hurt.

- Attending Mass and receiving Holy Communion are the most perfect and beautiful prayers our Church has to offer us, when they're available. Don't feel guilty if you can't get to Mass except on Sundays and Holy Days of Obligation. And certainly don't feel guilty if sickness or some other legitimate reason is keeping you from attending even Sunday Mass and Holy Days of Obligation regularly. If you're too sick to go to Mass, if you're incarcerated, if your car breaks down and you simply cannot make it, or if you're caring for a sick friend who can't be left unattended, Christ comes to be united with your suffering and brings you to heaven through the Mass anyway. You are still united to that prayer by grace and your own desire to be present.

- Please don't feel guilty if you're unable to attend daily Mass regularly. A lot of churches unfortunately don't offer daily Mass at convenient times for people who have to work and take care of children. While many children do fine being taken to daily Mass, there are also some times when it simply won't work out. However, if you can go to daily Mass, it's a wonderful blessing to do so. Perhaps you can resolve to go once a month on First Saturdays, or once a week on Fridays during lunch hour, or some other time that is open to you.

- The Divine Office, also known as Liturgy of the Hours, is the prayer offered by the Church at certain times every day. People pray it all over the world in monasteries and con-vents. Praying along with the Divine Office is a wonderful way to enter the prayer of the Church. You can pray the Divine Office using a book called the Breviary or by using an internet app such as the one offered by ibreviary.org, or a website such as divineoffice.org. Don't be intimidated by the number of prayers. It's great to start learning to pray the Divine Office by just offering Morning Prayer or Vespers every day, and then adding another prayer time once you get used to it.

- Try to make time for personal prayer as well as prayer at Mass and with the prayers of the Church. Take ten, twenty, or thirty minutes every day to just talk to God. I try to do this when I wake up in the morning. Talk with God about whatever's on your mind. Offer to him the people you're praying for and try to listen to what he is calling you to do.

- There's nothing wrong with making a list of people to pray for and rattling it off: "God bless Mother, God bless Dad, God Bless Aunt Betty," and so forth. But it's also perfectly fine to just tell God that you're interceding for everyone who has asked for your prayers and for those who have no one to pray for them, and let God remember who they are. God can keep track of everything, and we can't.

- By the great mercy of God, in a mysterious way I can't completely understand, we can even pray for the dead. The souls in purgatory are continuing the process God began in them on earth: the process of being healed and purified of sin so that they can enter heaven fully. This isn't God being a mean perfectionist. It's just that heaven is a perfect, complete place where everything invisible is made visible and everything is as it should be. If part of a person's heart is still attached to sin, they can't be in heaven until they've been healed of that. Think of purgatory as a hospital rather than a holdover jail. Somehow, when we pray for the dead, we relieve any way in which that healing is painful and help shorten their hospital stay. And when those souls go to heaven, they'll return the favor and pray for us as powerful advocates.

- Apart from canonized saints, we don't know who is in heaven yet, and we don't know if there's a single person in hell. So go ahead and pray for every person, living and dead. If they're already in heaven, they'll return the favor right away.

Prayer is a little, purposeful visit to heaven into the divine movement of the Holy Trinity. When we intercede for someone else,
we bring them with us and allow God's grace to work on them
in a new way. Prayer is not an excuse for inaction, nor is it better
than action. It's the foundation that should inform our action
in the first place, sustain it, and fill in what we cannot accom-
plish ourselves. When we perform this final spiritual Work of
Mercy, we are doing for the living and the dead what God does,
drawing them up into the fullness of grace.

Lord Jesus,
you eternally offer your prayer of gratitude
and love to the Father.
Thank you for the gift of prayer.
Help me to meet you in prayer faithfully.
Send your Holy Spirit through the gift of
    prayer,
to help me live the Works of Mercy all the days
    of my life.
I ask this in your most holy name.
Amen.

APPENDIX
LIST OF CHARITIES

In order to perform the Works of Mercy, you may want to use this list of the charities, organized by Work of Mercy, that I've mentioned in this book.

friendshiproom.net

The Friendship Room is a hospitality house operating in downtown Steubenville, Ohio. In addition to their website, you can donate to them and follow them on their Facebook page: https://www.facebook.com/friendshiproom/.

FEED THE HUNGRY

feedingamerica.org

Feeding America has a map and list of all the food banks in the United States, so you can donate money directly and find one near you.

GIVE DRINK TO THE THIRSTY

paperforwater.org

Paper for Water is a charity that digs wells to provide safe water for people who need it all over the world. It also provides education for children about the worldwide water crisis.

CLOTHE THE NAKED

beauty2thestreetz.org

Beauty 2 the Streetz is an organization that provides hygiene, meals, clothing, tents, makeovers, haircuts, and hair styling to the unhoused men and women on Skid Row in Los Angeles.

SHELTER THE HOMELESS

habitat.org

Habitat for Humanity is an organization that helps people in need all over the world to build their own homes.

VISIT THE IMPRISONED/ RANSOM THE CAPTIVE

innocenceproject.org

The Innocence Project seeks to exonerate wrongfully convicted people through DNA testing and criminal justice reform.

nominetwork.org

Nomi Network seeks to protect women from human trafficking through economic empowerment.

raicestexas.org

RAICES (Refugee and Immigrant Center for Education and Legal Services) provides legal representation for immigrants and refugees.

immigrantfamiliestogether.com

Immigrant Families Together works quickly to pay the bond for immigrants imprisoned at the southern border of the United States. They then raise money to get the immigrants housing, food, education, and medical care while they wait for their immigration hearing. They also provide legal representation.

Bury the Dead

childrensburial.org

Children's Burial Assistance provides financial assistance for needy families who have to bury a deceased child.

thetearsfoundation.org

The TEARS Foundation provides funeral financial assistance for parents who have lost a baby.

finalfarewell.org

Final Farewell assists families who have to bury a deceased child.

Mary E. Pezzulo is the creator of the *Steel Magnificat* blog on the *Patheos* Catholic channel, where she writes about everything from current events to movies to poverty in the Ohio Valley to the kindness of strangers.

Pezzulo earned a bachelor's degree in English from Otterbein University and studied philosophy at Franciscan University of Steubenville. She is the author of *Meditations on the Way of the Cross.*

She and her husband, Michael, live in Steubenville, Ohio, with their daughter.

www.patheos.com/blogs/steelmagnificat
Facebook: Steel Magnificat
Twitter: @mary_pezzulo